EI

MW01193727

"There is no greater joy than seeing your family love Jesus and love each other deeply. This book is a real-life guide to making that happen for your family."

Steve Dulin, Elder and Associate Senior Pastor
Gateway Church
Southlake, TX

"Don and Suzanne have written a clever, insightful, transparent, funny and altogether practical book on family, but more than that, they have written a book that honors and glorifies the God of the Bible and His intent for our joy in relationship to Him and to our families and beyond. I have known this family for over 25 years. Their deep insight and wisdom has been hard-earned and is a personal revelation of how the Gospel has the power to redeem every area of our lives. Reading this book will make you laugh, encourage you, challenge you, teach you and most importantly, give you hope as it points you to the source of all hope—Jesus Christ. I could not recommend it more."

Jeff Haley, Elder
The Village Church
Flower Mound, TX

"Don and Suzanne Manning have shaped much of how we approach parenting. They have shared their lives with us and our family continues to benefit from their wisdom and influence. Reading this book will be like inviting in the wisest mentors to sit down and walk you through life's most challenging yet rewarding season of life. Their wisdom will guide you to build the family relationships you've always hoped for."

Ben Moreno, Lewisville Campus Pastor
Valley Creek Church
Flower Mound, TX

"As parents, how often do we put more emphasis in the behavior of our children, all the while losing sight of the most important piece in their development, their heart. In Crazy Cool Family, Don and Suzanne Manning paint the picture of how connecting with their children's hearts create a culture where deep relationships thrive."

David and Ally Schreiner

"The Manning's teaching on family is truly life-changing. We are so thankful for their willingness to go deep with the Lord in family and parenting. The result is their lifetime of parenting wisdom available to us and a model for a Crazy Cool Family! If you have struggled to find answers to life's toughest questions about parenting and family—and what parent hasn't—then this book is for you."

Justin and Laura Milum

"The true testament to Don and Suzanne's parenting practices is the character and wisdom that each of their seven children possess. Their children are the type of people you want your own children to be influenced by. They are solid role models for our children."

Justin and Angie Seedorf

"We have personally learned so much from Don and Suzanne and have had the privilege of a front-row seat for 10+ years to this 'Crazy Cool Family.' We have seen Don and Suzanne love and lead countless other parents and we are so excited this resource is available! They have lived out the truths of this book and have given us a great example of how to raise our boys."

Josh and Rachael Wintermute

# Crazy Cool Family

## Rethink the Way You Do Family

DON and SUZANNE MANNING

Underscore Publ. USA
www.underscorepublishing.com

# DEDICATION

To Kevin and Lisa Evans, the couple that started us on our amazing family journey with Jesus.

And to all the parents who read this book. As Kevin and Lisa started us, may we start you toward your own amazing family journey with Jesus!

# CONTENTS

# FOREWORD

If you look into the eyes of a child, you will see the ultimate potential. Pressed into their soul is the very image and likeness of God. They were born with the ability to create, the capacity to love, the calling to lead, the heart to serve, and the desire for life. As parents, our calling is clear—to simply release what is already there.

Therefore, there is no greater responsibility than to raise children. And while that may feel overwhelming there is also no greater privilege than to raise children. John, the Apostle of love, said, *"I have no greater joy than to see my children walking in the truth"* (3 John 4). John reminds us that there is nothing greater in life than to see our kids discover who they are, who God is, and what they were created to do. Our hearts long to see our children live in the freedom of who they were created to be. True joy comes when we lay down our lives to help our kids become fully free. Our ceiling is meant to become their floor. That is the great responsibility and privilege of every parent.

We have been invited to partner with God to shape and mold the hearts and lives of the ones He has entrusted to us. Like the good Father has done for us, we are invited to protect and provide for their well-being, love and encourage their souls, forgive their failures and mistakes, connect with their hearts, declare their identities, and inspire them to greatness. Kingdom parenting is not about controlling the behavior of our children. It's about calling forth their destinies.

But how do we *actually* do that?

In today's world, it seems like it is harder than ever to be an effective parent. Culture, technology, and the systems of the world all seem to be working against us. The family feels like it is fractured now more than ever. For many of us, we don't know what healthy family even looks like. Many of us didn't have godly parents, and we aren't sure where to start. And while we may not know exactly how to raise our kids, God has entrusted them to us because He believes in us. God believes in you! God gave you your children because you are perfectly designed to release their fullest potential. In other words, you have everything you need to be a great parent; you just have to learn to lean into the ways of the kingdom. While the world tells us to control our children, demand them to perform, and expect the worst, the kingdom invites us to trust, extend grace, and believe the best. That is why *Crazy Cool Family* is such a timely book.

i

I have watched my friends, Don and Suzanne, model kingdom parenting as long as I have known them. They have a unique insight and a divine favor in building healthy families. As amazing parents with an amazing family, they have poured their years of experience and wisdom into this book for us. What I love about their approach is that it reflects how the Father parents us.

*Crazy Cool Family* is more than a book—it is a guide to help us become healthy parents who are raising healthy kids. Every chapter does something incredibly unique. It brings everything back to what matters most—the heart. *"Above all else guard your heart, for everything you do flows from it"* (Proverbs 4:23). *Crazy Cool Family* reminds us that parenting is simply about surrendering our heart to God while helping our kids' hearts become alive, whole, and free.

You may have picked up this book because you want some help in your parenting. And while it will help you learn how to lead your children, it will, more importantly, help you learn how to live with the freedom of a childlike heart. You are the Father's beloved son or daughter in whom He is well pleased—not because of what you have done but because of what Jesus has done. And loved sons become great fathers. And loved daughters become great mothers. The greatest thing you can do for your kids is to learn to live free as a beloved son or daughter because you can teach what you know, but you will always reproduce who you are. Kingdom parenting is the journey of learning to live as a beloved son or daughter while raising mighty men and women of God. It is the upside-down way of the kingdom. It is the upside-down way of Jesus. It is the journey of a *Crazy Cool Family!*

John Stickl
Lead Pastor, Valley Creek Church
Author of *Follow the Cloud*

## crazy
/krāzē/
*adjective*
*informal:* extremely enthusiastic
*synonyms:* passionate about, (very) keen on, enamored of, infatuated with, smitten with, devoted to

*Crazy as in:* "I have a crazy good connection with my kids!"

## cool
/ko͞ol/
*adjective*
*informal:* fashionably attractive or impressive
*synonyms:* fashionable, stylish, chic, up-to-the-moment, sophisticated

*slang:* very good
*synonyms:* awesome, amazing

*Cool as in:* "My family is so cool!"

# START HERE

There is one thing for certain about a house with seven kids—it's *crazy cool* on Christmas morning. Two girls sit laughing on the couch, looking at photos and videos from the night before. The boys are putting some new electronic toy together on the floor. Everyone else is in the kitchen preparing breakfast.

Organized chaos. So many presents. We have a tradition—each of our kids buys every one of their siblings a present. It doesn't always involve a lot of money. It really is *the thought that counts*. And each child opens every present with everyone watching. That's 49 presents, one at a time. And that's just sibling gifts.

Paper everywhere. "Save the bags! We reuse them!" someone calls out as we take a break to eat breakfast. Cinnamon rolls. Sausage. Muffins—regular and gluten-free. Eggs. Fruit. Conversation. Laughter.

One year, as we cleaned up breakfast, the kids started whispering about something. Then a couple of the girls snuck out and returned with a framed canvas with some writing on it. Our children had gotten together to compose a family mission statement and presented it to Suzanne and me.

Here's what it says: *"In this house, you'll find a family that chooses to love life. Where Jesus is our Friend, Father, and Savior. A place where dance parties are always welcome, and secrets are never kept. Where we stay up too late sitting at the* counter, *talking about life. A place where Mom washes the world off of us, and Dad prays us out the door. Where big sisters are sometimes moms, and little brothers are best friends. Where we find joy in just being together. We thank Jesus for our home and the people we share it with. This is what makes our house a home."*

I had tears in my eyes. As I looked around the room, I wasn't alone.

Later that day when Suzanne and I had a moment to ourselves, we reflected on the experience—we really do have a *Crazy Cool Family!*

What does *Crazy Cool Family* mean? It's the family Suzanne and I always dreamed of having when we started our lives together. A family which loves each other and truly enjoys being around each other. A family anchored by a fun, healthy marriage, and kids who are joyful and purposeful, making good choices in life. A family which loves Jesus, is growing in relationship with Him, and has crazy faith to both listen for God's voice and to follow Him.

That's a sweet picture, isn't it? With the Mannings, it really is a true picture. We're not perfect by any means, but somehow, by the grace of God, we have raised seven kids who love Jesus, love each other, and love us. It is *Crazy Cool.* That's the only way I know how to describe it.

I suspect we all start out with good and healthy expectations. Depending on your generation, you probably grew up watching families like the Bradys, Cunninghams, Partridges, Keatons, Seavers, and Tanners on television. Issues arose, but nothing that couldn't be resolved into a big family group hug by the end of a 30-minute episode.

It's not a very realistic picture, is it? More often than not, as our good and healthy expectations encounter real life, family can become a matter of holding on for dear life. Many families—even Christian families, people we are close to—struggle with unfulfilled marriages, broken relationships, teenage rebellion, and shattered family dreams. We see families, young and old, splintering all around us. Watching this scene play out over and over, I started to ask God, "How is it that some families have great relationships and great kids, and others don't? God, You know that we love You and we've always tried to be obedient. We've certainly not been perfect. We're still overcoming issues every day. But if You can do this for us with all our junk, then You can do it for anyone! We didn't start with anything special, but You have given us a family that is really special. Can You show us how to share what You've done in our lives with others?"

I asked, and God answered.

He started to download things to me. He reminded me of things He has taught us over the years. I'd write them down and go over it with Suzanne for her recollection. Much of it I'd learned from her originally anyway.

Over the years, as our family continued to grow and mature, we started teaching other parents what we'd learned. We've continued to hone the message God has given us, to simplify and clarify it. The great news in this game is that everyone can win. In fact, the more Crazy Cool Families there are out there, the more Crazy Cool our world becomes.

God was gracious enough to give us a taste of something different in our family. We've seen Him work in other families the same way. He has opened the door for us to teach hundreds of families how to have a Crazy Cool Family of their own. That's where you come in!

We don't believe you're holding this book in your hands by accident.

Jesus said, "Enter through the NARROW gate. For wide is the gate and broad is the way that leads to destruction, and many enter through it. But SMALL is the gate and NARROW the road that leads to life, and only a few find it" (Matthew 7:13-14, emphasis mine).

Jesus has this habit of what Suzanne calls "flipping your thinking." In this case, He invites us to find life by going with the few instead of the crowd. Our goal is the same in this book and in our ministry. Going with God to create a Crazy Cool Family will require you to flip your thinking on how to do family. You will definitely be going with the few instead of the crowd. As you'll see, God's ways really are crazy, but they are so, so cool when we start to see them clearly!

The result? Just a few chapters later, Jesus offers, *"Come to me, all you who are weary and burdened, and I will give you REST. Take my yoke upon you, and learn from me. For I am meek and lowly in heart, and you will find REST for your souls. For my yoke is EASY, and my burden is LIGHT"* (Matthew 11:28-30, emphasis mine).

What if family was restful? Not restful where everyone sleeps all the time—though we could all use more sleep—but rather peaceful. What if family was easy? Not easy as in lazy, but easy as in flowing; like a good golfer "makes it look easy." What if family was not a burden but felt light? A place where everyone found rest for their souls?

How is your family story playing out?

Suzanne and I have spent many years on our own Crazy Cool Family journey. The road God has shown us is definitely narrow but has been worth all we've invested. Today, family is the easiest thing in our lives, and besides His wonderful salvation, it's the very best gift He's ever given us.

How does that sound? We're living proof—it's all true. And it's our privilege—a real blessing for us—to have this opportunity to encourage you on the path to your own *Crazy Cool Family!*

Are you ready?

**fam·i·ly**
/fam(ə)lē/
noun
1.  a group consisting of parents and children living together in a household
2.  all the descendants of a common ancestor

*"A happy family is but an earlier heaven."*
                                                    —George Bernard Shaw

*For he issued his laws to Jacob; he gave his instructions to Israel. He commanded our ancestors to teach them to their children. So the next generation might know them—even the children not yet born—and they in turn will teach their own children. So each generation should set its hope anew on God, not forgetting his glorious miracles and obeying his commands.*
                                                    —Psalm 78:5-7 NLT

# 1

---

## THE PATH TO A CRAZY COOL FAMILY

It's ironic, really. For all the magnificent advances of our fast-paced, high-tech society, for all the short-cuts and life-hacks discovered, all the state-of-the-art tools and toys at our disposal, we're all doing a lot more, but accomplishing a lot less. And the effect of all of this on the family? Life moves at a blistering pace, we all get caught up in its stride, and family interactions start to resemble ships passing in the night. If and when we ever do find ourselves in the same place at the same time, we don't know how to relate.

Moms and dads are left wanting for anything more than one-word answers from their teens; teens long for one interaction where their parents will listen to them and not be critical; siblings are ready to rumble over every little thing. Today's coping mechanism? Everyone in the house retreats to the devices designed—and marketed—to connect us, but which really serve to isolate. Smartphones, video games, social media—everyone goes nose-to-screen.

Sound familiar? You're not alone. For many, *this* is family life.

# Is *This* All There Is?

Where is God in our families? Does the abundant life He promises us in John 10:10 apply to families? When Jesus said, *"I have come that they may have life and have it to the full,"* was there a disclaimer which I'd never heard that reads, except for in your family, where you're doomed for busyness and *mediocrity?* God is so good, and yet, take a look around. Families are in peril everywhere you look. Confusion, discouragement, frustration, disappointment, and desperation— there has to be something more! There is.

If you look up "how to improve your life" on the web and social media, you'll find a lot of lists. Things like *Top Ten* of this or that, *Five Things to do on a Saturday with the family, Three Steps to a better quiet time, Eight Ways to be more productive.* We human beings are always looking for a quick fix because we are drowning, and we think maybe, just maybe, some additional information will improve our situation.

In Matthew 22, Jesus was asked what was most important about life. His list was two things, but neither is a quick fix. "He said, *'Love the Lord your God with all your heart and with all your soul and with all your mind.' This is the first and greatest commandment. And the second is like it: 'Love your neighbor as yourself'"* (Matthew 22:37-40).

In His simple, yet profound style, Jesus said the most

*Information is not going to give us a Crazy Cool Family. Relationships will.*

important thing in life is *relationships.* He is abundantly clear. First, we focus on our relationship with our Heavenly Father. We love God with everything we have. This first key relationship creates a healthy self, who can then love others in a healthy way—loving others as we would want to be loved.

Information is not going to give us a Crazy Cool Family. Relationships will.

Throughout this book, you are going to see what we call Crazy Cool Concepts (CCCs). These statements are like very powerful tweets—short statements we hope will go deep in your heart. Here's the first one:

STRONG FAMILIES ARE BUILT ON STRONG RELATIONSHIPS

## The Foundation of a Crazy Cool Family

More than anything else, God is a god of relationships. You see it in His very nature—He is both singular and plural. He is one God, existing in fellowship, Father, Son, and Holy Spirit. We get a hint of this from the very beginning, where we read, *"In the beginning God created the heavens and the earth"* (*Genesis 1:1*). God is called Elohim—a Hebrew word singular in sense, and plural in form. And again, later in the creation narrative, where God counsels with Himself, *"Let us make mankind in our image, in our likeness"* (*Genesis 1:26*).

If you want to go back even further than that, look at John 1:1—*"In the beginning was the Word and the Word was with God and was God."* The Trinity was there even before the creation of the world. God has been in relationship for eternity.

You and me, and our spouses and children, were all created in His image and likeness, both singular and to exist in relationship with God and others.

In 1 John 4:8, we see that the essence of God is love. And Jesus, as He was preparing to leave His disciples—among His last words to them before His arrest, trial, and the cross—instructed, *"Love each other as I have loved you"* (John 15:12). In other words, embody your identity as a child of God. Be relational.

God could have created us any way He wanted. He could have dropped mature adults from the sky, delivered by storks to the earth from heaven. He could have kept us from aging and have everyone remain the same all their lives. He could have made all of us look the same, think the same, and act the same so we would get along better.

But He didn't. He started us out as defenseless infants, bound to and needing the care of parents. He made us all different, and each unique. He made us as beings who age, get sick, and have issues. He gave us a heart that has free will to move towards or away from God, and each other.

He could have called Himself anything, but He chose to call Himself our Father.

God designed us to be in relationships, and He designed us to be in families. We learn from the relationship of Jesus to His Father not only how we are to relate to God, but how as parents we are to relate to children, and how as children, we are to relate to parents.

The depth and quality of relationships to God and to family members are absolutely critical to pursue in our families. It's built into us. It's in our DNA. It's our identity—who we are and who we're to be.

Pursuing relationships within your family is key. A Crazy Cool Family strives for more—far more—than peaceful coexistence. It's about real intimacy, genuine and authentic love.

The narrow road to a family that is easy, restful, and light is through relationships. When relationships are strong, kids obey better, everyone gets along better, everyone is more open to Jesus, and family is more engaging and fun.

*God's narrow road for family is actually a relational journey.*

God's narrow road for family is actually a relational journey. When we pursue relationships first, everything else falls into place.

So how do we do family relationships? That's what this book is all about!

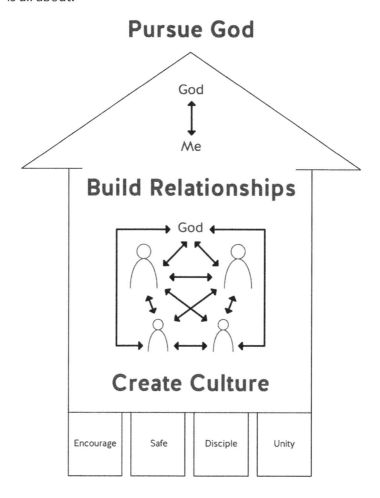

## Pursue God

God

Me

## Build Relationships

God

## Create Culture

| Encourage | Safe | Disciple | Unity |

## The Big Picture

It's important to understand how this book is written and how we recommend you use it to transform your family. Mark this page so you can come back to this section as you read through the book. I know bookmarking is all different now with printed and digital books—remember when we could just dog-ear a page? Do whatever you have to so you can quickly refer back to this section.

Just like family is relational and our Bible is a book of stories, this book is written to be relational as well. We're not showing you techniques, but a way of life! But in all the stories and the concepts, that picture is sometimes easily lost. We want you to have a map to refer back to at all times. Remember, this journey is years in the making.

The illustration on the previous page is our map. We'll return to this illustration throughout the book, with different sections highlighted to help show you where you are. But this is a great time and place to introduce you to the big picture. Come back to it as often as needed to stay grounded.

As you can see in the illustration, there are three statements that summarize all we teach:

1. Pursue God
2. Build Relationships
3. Create Culture

Everything we talk about will be an extension of those three statements. Why are these three themes so vitally important? Let me quickly break it down:

# Pursue God

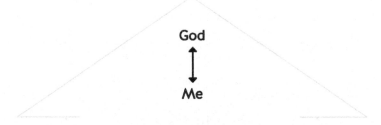

At the top of the house is our connection to God. It's at the top and singled out because it's the most important relationship you have in the family. From your perspective— and you are the one we are talking to, the one reading this book—the best thing you can do for your family is have a God-connected, healthy version of yourself.

Jesus said in Matthew 12:34, *"The mouth speaks what the heart is full of."* What your heart is full of overflows into your family. Spiritually growing, healthy parents create spiritually growing, healthy families. In Section One, we are going to consider why your relationship with God is so important to our family and reveal some key characteristics of a fruitful connection with God.

# Build Relationships

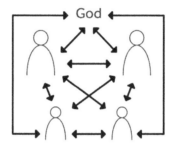

At the center of our illustration and the center of the Crazy Cool Family home is the network of relationships. We have drawn a very traditional family—a husband, wife, and two kids—into our cool illustration, but you should draw your family into the box. Ours only fits if we draw it really small!

In Section Two, we're going to show you how to see family through the network of its relationships. The strength of your family will be directly related to the strength of its relationships. True obedience and God-oriented achievement will only happen when the family is connected to God and each other. When you understand the way relationships impact your family, it will change the way you interact with your family forever.

Even if I've never met you, I know something about your family. I know that they are amazing! How do I know that if we've never met? Because I know Who created them!

Psalm 139:13-15 says, *"For you created my inmost being, you knit me together in my mother's womb. I praise you because I am fearfully and wonderfully made; your works are wonderful, I know that full well. My frame was not hidden from you when I was made in the secret place, when I was woven together in the depths of the earth."*

News flash! Your job as a parent isn't to make your kids amazing. They already are. Your job is to work with God to bring out the amazingness that is already in them. And that amazingness is brought out through relationship. If relationship is most important to Jesus, it should be most important to us.

Look at all the relational lines in our Crazy Cool Family home. We are going to spend a chapter on every relational aspect in our homes: Our relationship to God, the marriage relationship, parents' relationship to kids, kids' relationship to Jesus, and kids' relationships to each other.

As go these relationships, so goes the family. When every relational line is strong, the family is strong.

## Create Culture

| Encourage | Safe | Disciple | Unity |

Finally, the foundation of our Crazy Cool Family home is its culture. One definition of culture is "the behaviors and beliefs characteristic of a particular group." In this case, our "group" is the family. The culture in our home primarily consists of the behaviors and beliefs put into the home by the parents.

We get so many parents coming to us frustrated and complaining about the toxic culture in their home. No one wants to be there due to the tension and expectations that are constant sources of pressure. We get to show them how they've created the very culture they can't stand. Fun stuff! No.

It really isn't very fun at first, but as they start to understand, they realize God has given us great, great influence over the culture or the atmosphere of our own home. Then these parents start to work to change the very culture that is bothering them so much.

What's your family culture? What do you want it to be? Is anger part of the culture or joy? Is the culture perfectionist or lackadaisical? Is sports or music or hunting or academics a big part of the culture? What's important in the culture? Finally, and maybe most important, does your family culture make you want to come home... or go somewhere else?

In Section Three, our aim is to help you create a culture in which all of your family relationships can flourish. That will make home your family's favorite place to be. Over time, we have honed the culture message down to four fundamental aspects of the family that we believe are essential to a Crazy Cool Family. But I'm getting ahead of myself. One step at a time.

This book builds from conceptual to practical. We have to build the relational framework in your mind and heart before we can fill in and flesh out the practical.

So stay with us as we move down through this illustration. We start with your relationship with God, move on to all the relationships in the family, and finish with creating a foundational culture in your home that brings out the best in everyone in your family!

## Family Impact

When Suzanne and I sit down with parents to talk about their family, one of the first things we tell them is what I am about to put in a CCC:

> YOU WILL HAVE A MAJOR IMPACT ON YOUR FAMILY.
> YOUR ONLY CHOICE IS WHAT THAT IMPACT WILL BE.

Whether family is done well or poorly, family has a major impact on our lives. I don't know anyone—not anyone—who has not been heavily influenced by their upbringing. If a dad has left the home, the child has to deal with abandonment issues. If a mom was very demanding, the child has to deal with never feeling like he or she was good enough. If a family loses a child, everyone in the family will deal with that issue for the rest of their lives.

On the other side, parents who have a stable marriage provide great stability for their children. The parent who believes in their child will give that child such confidence. A strong bond between siblings will bring a lifetime of friendship.

As adults, we can all look back and see the very significant influence of our parents and siblings—both good and bad—in shaping our lives. Family impacts you, influences you, shapes you.

This book is about helping you make your impact be the best it can be. For Suzanne and me, that's what our whole lives and ministry are about—*encouraging and helping you discover how to build your own Crazy Cool Family.*

Are you ready to get started? Before we do, Suzanne and I have two really important thoughts to share with you:

*Don't be overwhelmed.* Creating a Crazy Cool Family takes time. This book is not a series of parenting tips. It is quite literally a way of life. It will take years of changing your belief systems and working through the different stages of family life to see the full fruits of your family labor.

*Don't be discouraged.* We've seen time and again in speaking to many, many parents, wading into this material can cause you to think you've done everything wrong, your family is doomed to failure, and all hope is lost. That's absolutely not the case. James 4:7 applies here. It says, *"Submit yourselves, then, to God. Resist the devil and he will flee from you."*

Be encouraged! If you are reading this book, it's because you care deeply about your family and you want God's best for everyone in it. You're setting out on a lifetime journey to allow our incredible Heavenly Father to lead you in creating a Crazy Cool Family you will enjoy for the rest of your life.

**SUZANNE:** One of my favorite things to do is encourage families as they fight the good fight. Here is a CCC for you:

> YOU ARE THE BEST PARENT FOR YOUR CHILDREN. GOD CHOSE YOU TO BE THEIR PARENT. IT WAS NO ACCIDENT!

You've been hand-picked by God to be your children's parent. You love and want what's best for them—more than anyone else in the world. You've been given every good gift that you need to train your children up in the way they should go. You know them and all their little quirks just like our Father knows us. And lastly, you have the Creator of the universe on your side—as your helper. Use HIM!

Just take one step at a time. Right now, that step is opening this book, looking to understand more about God, yourself, and your family. You won't get it all overnight. At least I didn't. God just kept peeling back the layers and letting me see more and more of His heart and the hearts of my family. But the journey has given me the family of my dreams.

And our family is so excited to share more with you!

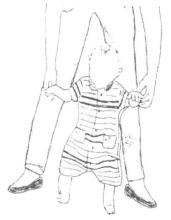

*One step at a time.*

## to·geth·er
/təˈgeT͟Hər/
*adverb*

1. with or in proximity to another person or people
*synonyms:* with each other, in conjunction, jointly, in cooperation, in collaboration, in partnership, in combination, in league, in tandem, side by side, hand in hand, shoulder to shoulder.

2. at the same time
synonyms: simultaneously, at the same time, at once, all together, as a group, in unison, in concert, in chorus, as one, with one accord.

*"The family—that dear octopus from whose tentacles we never quite escape, nor, in our inmost hearts, ever quite wish to."*
—Dodie Smith, Author of 101 Dalmatians.

*"You don't choose your family. They are God's gift to you, as you are to them."*
—Desmond Tutu

*For this reason I kneel before the Father, from whom every family in heaven and on earth derives its name. I pray that out of his glorious riches he may strengthen you with power through his Spirit in your inner being, so that Christ may dwell in your hearts through faith.*
—Ephesians 3:14-17

# 2

---

## OUR FAMILY TO YOURS

With seven children, the Manning family is numerous if nothing else. It's funny to see people's reaction to our large family. Let me go ahead and get these out of the way—

No, we're not Mormons. No, we're not Catholic. Yes, we do know what causes this. Seriously, people ask us those questions all the time!

We didn't really set out to have a large family in the beginning. At least I didn't. Suzanne later confessed she was a fan of 70s TV shows like Eight is Enough, The Brady Bunch, and The Partridge Family—all shows with big families. We met some families who had a lot of children which opened us up to the possibilities. But really, it just kind of happened one child at a time. I guess God thought we needed a lot of parenting training or as Suzanne likes to put it, we needed sanctifying so we didn't get to stop with just two or three kids.

A large family certainly makes things different. We usually drive on vacations instead of flying. Eating out costs a whole lot more. We're never lacking for things to do or events to attend. And we'll never, ever be finished paying for colleges and weddings. We keep dropping them off at college, but then there are always more at home. And it doesn't look like we will get that empty-nester gap between kids leaving home and grandkids coming. Grandkids are on the horizon and we still have a middle schooler! Oh well. Good thing we like kids! Other than just *more of everything*, the Mannings are a pretty normal family. We have pets, we love sports, we go to church, we eat out too much, we spend too much money, and our kids are on their electronics way too often. Our kids' rooms are not always clean, and they don't always do everything we want them to do. Sound familiar?

## Meet the Mannings

People ask me, "How can you have seven kids?" I tell them I have a great wife.

Even though I'm doing the bulk of this writing, this work is really a joint effort with my wonderful, beautiful bride, Suzanne. We've been married for more than a quarter-century. At times, as you've seen, she'll jump in with her own specific thoughts to share, but rest assured, everything I write is from her as well. Suzanne has an awesome passion and energy for life and family—it's contagious.

*My children are my favorite people in the whole world.*

**SUZANNE: I feel like it's important for you to hear why we decided to write a book on parenting. It's not because we are perfect parents, or we've read hundreds of parenting books (we've read our share), or our children are flawless. Not at all. We've written this book because we have a passion for you as a parent!**

**I tell people all the time my children are my favorite people**

in the whole world. If you were to give me a day free of responsibility, I would choose to spend it with my children, either all together or one-on-one. They bless my life with their words, actions, and their very being. They are smart, fun, beautiful, and spiritual. They make me laugh, touch me to tears, and bless my soul daily. I feel honored, privileged, and blessed beyond words that I get to be their parent. Can you say that about your children? Do you? If you don't, then this book is for you. And if you do already feel and believe that about your children, then this book will especially affirm and resonate with you!

See what I mean? Suzanne really loves our family and has helped shape us all into people she loves to be around. Let me give you a CCC that connects with what she just said:

> CRAZY COOL FAMILIES CHOOSE TO BE TOGETHER. THEY ENJOY EACH MEMBER OF THE FAMILY.

As I mentioned, you'll also be hearing from our children. Our oldest daughter, Mollie, has been a huge help in writing and in motivating us to finish this book. She's the best *oldest kid* we could ever ask for or imagine! I've asked her to introduce the kids in her own unique way, but first, a little background on Suzanne and me to set the stage. I'll let Suzanne fill you in:

**SUZANNE: I always wanted a big family. I watched TV shows, created large Barbie families, and had several dolls I practiced being a mom to as a kid. I started babysitting in the 4th grade and, throughout the years, helped lots of families raise their children as their nanny. But when I became pregnant as a junior in college, my world was rocked. I saw my white picket fence dreams shattered. I wasn't ready to build a family yet. I waffled back and forth between keeping the baby or not, marrying or not. I was surrounded by family and friends that supported my decisions; I chose to keep and raise the baby, but not to get**

married. Although I loved Mollie's dad (we were high school sweethearts), I knew we would not be the best together, especially raising a child. *A side note: He went on to marry the perfect lady, they have two sons, and live 30-minutes away. Mollie has a great relationship with them.*

I lived at my dad's home, raised Mollie, finished college, became a 6th-grade teacher... and went on way too many blind dates.

You see, when friends and family see a single mom they are desperate to get that woman a husband and the baby a daddy. I have to admit I agreed! I had started the big family plan without the husband/daddy...not good! It was lonely, hard, scary... just to name a few feelings. But I was done with the blind dates, so I made a deal with God I would go on one more blind date and then I would put this whole dating thing on hold for a while. It was just too hard being a part of the dating scene while raising an infant. That last blind date was with Don.

His long-time friend's wife and I taught at the same school. And she had "the perfect person" for me. She was right. I walked into their house, saw Don across the room, and very clearly heard God's voice saying, "you will marry him in a year." While I knew we would be a family, it took Don a little longer to warm up to the "instant family" idea. We spent that whole year getting to know each other, Don practicing being a dad. At the end of that year, he proposed down on one knee, in a limo, with tons of roses and a beautiful princess cut diamond ring. I said yes...and so did Mollie!

So, it was a package deal for me! I like to say that I met Mollie and married her mom! We were an instant family and I was good with that. Mollie was a two-year-old and just a little less mature than Suzanne and I at that time! Our family grew from there. I'll let Mollie tell you more.

MOLLIE: My parents have a pretty cool story, right? I love it. Might not be the picturesque romance one might assume about someone writing a parenting book, but it shows great redemption, great pursuit, and great love—all of which have given me a very real picture of what it looks like to be redeemed, pursued, and loved by a God who is also a father.

If your story isn't the white picket fence you dreamed of, be encouraged; something amazing *will* result because we serve a very good Father. What was my parents' *something amazing*? Well, seven children of course! Seven children that all have names starting with the letter M. Yes, we thought it was weird too, and no, we don't know why they did it.

I am the oldest. My first little sister, Madeline, was born when I was four and a half, and after that, they came very quickly. My mom was pregnant or nursing for 15 years of my life—yes, I laugh when I read that too! Macy was born 18 months later, making Madeline a big sister and giving her quite the little baby doll. I saved Macy's life at least a dozen times that first year. McKenzie was born when Macy was two. (Are you counting in your head?) Don had four daughters in his first five years of marriage all under the age of seven. Yes, I'm laughing again, too.

But not to worry, as Mom put in his birth announcement, the all-girl Manning team went co-ed! Michael joined the crew when McKenzie was two and a half, and we were finished, whew, done! Just kidding. Maddox, whose name is by far the coolest, we all agree, was born when I was 14. Can you do that math? How old was everyone else? Basically, there were a lot of children... who cares about the ages?! But why stop now, two boys in a row, more please. On a family vacation in Colorado, Mom and Dad pulled us aside and said they had something to tell us—I was the only one of the six that thought it meant we were getting extra souvenir money. McCade, our baby, the perfect ending to the many Mannings was born in 2006. I lost track of the math and don't even really remember everyone's age, ever, but there we are. Mollie, Madeline, Macy, McKenzie, Michael, Maddox, McCade—and yes, our parents do call us the Many Mannings. You could say my parents had their hands full—of dirty diapers, boogers, messy rooms, and whining, but also of memories, baby giggles, bedtime stories, and lots and lots of parenting advice.

Can't you just feel the energy coming from her as she writes? Mollie writes just like she talks—in constant motion. Whatever she loves—or hates for that matter—she does with passion and clarity. Ask her about celebrating the Fourth of July or her favorite restaurant, and you will get a detailed and passionate response. Her excitement for life mirrors her passion for the Lord.

**SUZANNE: Mollie did a great job introducing you to the Manning family. Throughout this book, the kids will add their perspectives on different topics, so I'd like to introduce each child's different qualities to help you grasp where they are coming from.**

**Mollie is the typical firstborn. She is type-A and has everything together with an excellent plan which she has the total energy to**  **execute. She is great with words, an extrovert, and loves to connect with people. She's very good at making people feel special, especially by buying them gifts. She loves Jesus with every ounce of her being and is quick to share His greatness with everyone. My story that sums up Mollie's personality is from when she was a toddler. She wanted her doll's blanket to be laid out on the floor, smooth with no wrinkles, but her coordination and little arms couldn't make it happen. She would be very unhappy until all the kinks were out. She wanted everything to be perfect for her baby doll and her world. She always sees the cup as potential, ready to be filled with many clever options.**

**Madeline is actually another firstborn because of the four years difference and her being Don's first child. She has**

a sweet deal because she doesn't carry the responsibility of the firstborn, but has the vision and leadership of it. Madeline is a chaotically organized person. She can pull off  any event with great success, but her room and her car are usually a mess. then Madeline walks into a room, it lights up with the love and power of Jesus in her. She walks in God's abundant favor. She's an extrovert, and her love language is quality time, so she cannot get enough of people. My story that sums up Madeline comes from when she was on a mission trip in China as a pre-teen, facing hikes up some crazy trails. Her first response was to sing Miley Cyrus' song, *The Climb*. She chooses to bring joy into every situation. She always sees the cup as overflowing.

Macy is in the middle and worked hard when she was young to not be in her big sisters' shadows. They both had such big personalities. Macy hit her stride in middle school when she discovered all her crazy talents: great sense of humor, gift for music, hard- working, sensitive and discerning, love for Jesus, and most importantly, she learned how to hear God's voice; He filled her with identity and purpose. She pursues God with reckless abandon. My story that sums up Macy is when she went on a road trip to D.C. with her aunt and cousins. She was torn between having an adventurous, great time and missing home and her mom. She shares her emotions  in a beautiful way. She is half introvert, half extrovert. Macy is quick to fill her cup, pour it out for others, and fill it up again.

McKenzie is a true middle child—three sisters before her and three brothers after her. But she doesn't act like a middle child at all. She is much more like a baby sister. She is free to be whoever she wants. She is kind, sensitive, thoughtful, and so very patient. She is a crazy extrovert, and completely focused on pulling people to Jesus. McKenzie seems to have unlimited capacity to love people well. She does this by asking questions and being  genuinely interested in their lives. My story on Kenz is when she was in high school, she prayed and prayed for a group of friends in her grade to choose God things. When they did, she cried as she told them how she'd been praying for six years for them. She makes such a huge impact on everyone she meets. Kenzie sees two cups, so she always has one to share.

Now the boys.

Although Michael is born fifth in the line-up, he is our first boy and exhibits all the leadership traits of a firstborn. He is an internal processor and introvert which makes him a man of few words. He's not shy but doesn't often share his opinion. He never talks bad about anyone. He has crazy discernment and is very mature (as you might imagine a boy would be after being raised by five women). Michael naturally draws people to Jesus through his reverence and respect for the Lord. My story on Michael is when he was little, I bought him a boy toy everywhere we went—you can imagine all the girl stuff with which he was surrounded. A matchbox car or a ball at the grocery store, a Batman or a Superman figure at Walmart—you get the picture. Michael wasn't a brat and never  asked for things, but what it did was build a belief for him that he is worth it, anything is possible, and his needs are taken care of with abundance. Now, that's how he approaches everything... that he is going to benefit and succeed. He is super confident. He doesn't have a cup at all. No need. The world is a giant cup, filled with the best that God has.

Maddox is another middle. You know you have a large

family when you have multiple firstborns, middles, and babies! Maddox is a great big brother to McCade. We all  agree he has done the most raising of Cade, and he's done a great job. Maddox is so kind and sensitive, thoughtful and brave. He's great at basketball and works on his shots and moves all the time. He has the best sense of humor, and he makes us laugh constantly. Maddox has a faith that is beyond his years. My story about Maddox is from one Christmas; we'd decided not to get McCade what he really wanted. Maddox came to us and said, "Don't get me anything." And then he gave us all the money he had saved up and said, "Use this to get Cade his gift." He does stuff like that all the time. Maddox takes his cup and shares it with whoever is in need.

Finally, McCade, the true baby! I have to share the story that at this point, I was so done with the M names. I don't recommend naming all your children using the same letter, so don't start. Mix it up from the beginning. I really wanted to name him William, but none of the family would let me. They said he would feel left out! McCade is the perfect last child for our family. He lets his sisters smother him with affection, and he lets his brothers pick on him without crying. He's smart and so independent. He's adventurous but cautious. He loves to climb on our roof with his buddy, but they stay in one spot. McCade's relationship with the Lord is in the process of becoming his own. He is so perceptive, and he sees the value of obedience. My story about McCade comes from when he was born. As soon as I saw him, I declared, "Oh, I love him!" And that has been the banner over his life. He walks in full confidence and security that he is loved. He's a prophet, and he sees the cup as black or white—and not much in between.

As I'm sure you will agree, children are all different. It is so fun to see their unique personalities emerge. What would you write about your kids?

## Be You, Not Us

Every so often over the years—I know you've seen it too—some book or course or teaching comes along and takes the church community by storm. All of a sudden, everyone is out to emulate the author or follow the model, with largely disappointing results. Like a religious fad, they come and go.

In *Experiencing God*, Henry Blackaby tells a story about a church that had a bus ministry. This congregation was so successful with their bus ministry they wrote a book about it. In no time, other churches had read the book and started their own bus ministry. Most were complete failures. Why? They hadn't heard from God to start a bus ministry. They'd just copied someone else's formula. For the church that had such a successful bus ministry, God put the wind in those sails! It was His unique plan for that particular church. Those who read it should have been inspired to look to the Lord for *His unique plan for their church*, rather than getting caught up in someone else's calling.

*God has designed your family uniquely. And that's good!*

Your path to a Crazy Cool Family is not a one-size-fits-all, copy-this-formula-to-a-T endeavor. God has designed your family uniquely. And that's good! Through this book, He wants to inspire you to find *His unique vision for your family*. While I trust there are many, many things you will find helpful in this book, realize it will show up in your family in God's own unique way. This is definitely not a follow-the-Manning-blueprint manual.

**SUZANNE: In the beginning, I watched other families and thought, I want my family to be just like that. But as God added each unique child to the mix, our family quickly took its own form. All the pieces were so different and so intricately woven together that it was impossible to be any other family than the exact one God designed for us. So rest in the idea that you have the best, perfect family for you!**

Our family certainly didn't follow a blueprint. People always ask us how we got to seven kids, and we really don't have an answer. I guess you could say we loosely planned for some of the kids and others... not so much.

When Madeline was about nine, she definitely had a plan. She decided five kids were not enough for the Manning household, and we should have another baby. Her real motivation was she loved babies and wanted a real baby girl doll to play with. She had always loved babies, and it was really cute to watch her—now don't freak out, moms, we *watched her*—at nine-years-old with a baby on her hip like a real mom.

One day as we prayed before dinner, she spoke up and said, "I'll pray!" We agreed and she offered up a one-line prayer: "Lord, help us have a baby. Amen!" Say what? At this point, we already had five kids—four girls and a boy. We were in no way thinking we would have another baby. We blew off the prayer as the silly wishes of a nine-year-old girl.

*"I'll pray!"*

**MADELINE: Not silly wishes at all! I loved babies and I knew God answered prayers. I knew if I asked Him, He would answer, so I just kept asking until He did. (I can be very persistent.) I loved playing dolls, but I loved real babies even more. I just knew life would the best if I had a real baby to play with and love.**

The prayers didn't stop. Every day for a year—*I'm not kidding*—in every prayer she was involved in with the family, she prayed the same one-line prayer. Every mealtime, bedtime, same thing. It became a family joke.

Well, one night God was given the smallest of opportunities—you can interpret that as a lack-of-protection opportunity—and what do you know? Nine months later, here comes Maddox! When Madeline found out we'd be having another boy, she cried all day because she had expected her prayers to be answered with a girl baby. (Those are so much more fun to dress up.)

To finish off our family—*seven IS the number of completion*—God knew Maddox needed a brother. To say we were surprised by McCade would be quite an understatement, but now we have no idea how we would ever do life without him. We recognize that even though we didn't think we'd have any more children, God had other ideas. He gave us the desire, acceptance, effort, and energy to have a large family.

We had to find God's unique vision for our family, and we are confident He will show you yours.

## How Many Kids?

We get this question a lot: "How many kids should we have? I don't think we could handle seven!"

The fact that we have a large family doesn't mean God designed every couple who reads this book to have a large family, and I believe I can hear many whooping and hollering in relief right now! That may or may not be God's plan for you. I will say this: We have seen many families open up to having more children, and I believe God has blessed them in it.

**SUZANNE: When people ask my opinion on how many kids they should have, I laugh and answer "Not seven!" Just kidding! I say two is easy because it's one-on-one. Three gets a little harder. But if you really want to have a reason to depend on God, have four or more children! Make life crazy fun and totally dependent on someone bigger and wiser than yourself!**

The impact of a big family was a little different for each of the kids. Madeline and Mollie share their perspectives:

**MADELINE: When asked if I like being one of seven, I get this child-like grin on my face and answer with an "OH MY GOSH, YES!" Despite the constant noise, the always empty pantry, the endless sporting events on weekends, and people's faces when they find out how many siblings you have... I still love it. Actually, I loved it so much that the most difficult part of college was leaving and not being able to be at home with my siblings. Growing up, there was never a day that I didn't have someone to play with or someone to take care of. Every time our parents sat us down with "big news," we always knew it was another baby. For months, the excitement would grow and then finally another baby was born, and it always made life more fun.**

Every baby born was a new adventure. Madeline was always game for more babies. For her, the more people in the family to hang out with, the better. But on the back end of that, with each baby, time with Mom and Dad got divided even farther. Although she loved her siblings, she also really valued time with us. I believe there were several times in her growing up years when she wished to hang out with one of us, and we couldn't make it happen. Definitely one of the many costs of being one of many.

**MOLLIE: Just to mix it up, I thought I would share a dark side of me. When Mom and Dad originally were having**

babies, I was too young to notice the changes it made in our lives. It slowly started to dawn on me as I got older, as the responsibilities grew, and with every new baby, I slowly started to resent what it meant to be a part of a big family. For example, when they told us about Maddox, I was 14, going into my freshman year. I had just gotten home from summer camp, high on life and Jesus, and "Guess what! We are going to have a baby!" My bags were still packed, and I told my parents I was moving in with my best friend. Fast forward a couple of years, going into my junior year of high school, "Guess what! We're pregnant!" I cried out of anger and frustration. My thoughts were selfish and self- indulgent. When Mom was pregnant, I was in charge. It was my job to clean, to fold laundry. I felt responsible for the upkeep of the house and the other kids. When she had the baby, the responsibilities multiplied because not only was Mom out, but there was a new baby which meant "Be quiet" and "Don't mess with Mom" and "Mom can't do this, can you?" And while all of this pressure was mostly my own doing, it was still something I chose to believe instead of experiencing the joy of a new life. 100% the opposite of Madeline, yeah?

However, the Lord in His redeeming power opened my eyes to the absolute joy of my siblings. I always loved them immensely, but I think it was when they brought McCade home that it finally dawned on me. I was sitting on my parents' bed, and he was lying in my lap. He was so tiny, and honestly the cutest thing I'd ever seen. His breath smelled like honeysuckle, and his eyes were happy. I thought, "You're my little brother! God gave you to us! I feel so absolutely honored to be your oldest sister." I wish I would have realized this sooner. Perhaps I would have loved the others in a more Christ-like manner. However, the Lord's mercy is new each day, and the love He has given me for their lives, for their success, the sympathy for them in their failures is a love I can only describe as a gift from the Lord. I love being a part of a big family, and I would never trade a single thing.

*"You're my little brother!
God gave you to us!"*

So how many kids for you? Ask the Lord. We took Psalm 127:3-5 seriously when it said, *"Children are a heritage from the Lord, offspring a reward from him. Like arrows in the hands of a warrior are children born in one's youth. Blessed is the man whose quiver is full of them."*

Here is one final point: We frequently meet parents who wish they had more kids, but we've never talked to a parent who said they had too many. Be open to God's leading and see what Crazy Cool blessings He brings to you!

With our large family, one thing we do bring to the table is experience. We've discovered a great many things that work. We've also made just about every mistake in the book, and we have a lot to share from that side of the table, too. Suzanne and I don't pretend to know everything there is to know about family life. There are many situations we haven't seen and many experiences we haven't had. But we're in the process of raising seven children who love the Lord, love their parents, and love each other.

The key is to not follow a method but to learn to open up to God's leading for your family. As you do that, you will begin to see God's unique design for your family emerge. He will put hopes and dreams for your family into your heart, and you will, over time, start to see these dreams come to life in your family. It's so cool!

So here you have the Mannings: Don, Suzanne, Mollie, Madeline, Macy, McKenzie, Michael, Maddox, and McCade. Four girls, then three boys. At the time of this writing, Mollie is 28 and McCade is 11. We have two out of college and married, yet still have one in fifth grade. Many of the parents of our older children's friends are empty nesters, while we are like grandparents to the parents of McCade's friends. Sometimes we dream about what it would be like to be empty nesters, but most of the time we're excited to live a full life with a definitely full family.

Now that you've met our crew, let's get started creating a Crazy Cool Family!

# Pursue God

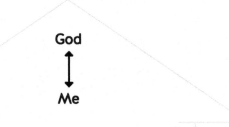

**God**

↑
↓

**Me**

Build Relationships

God

Create Culture

Encourage    Safe    Disciple    Unity

# SECTION ONE: PURSUE GOD

Most parenting books are primarily about how to get better behavior from your kids. If not better behavior, then at least better ways to control that behavior.

Yet we start with a section called "Pursue God." Why? Simple, really. The best thing we will do for our family isn't learning better behavior or control techniques. The best thing we will do for our families is to pursue God with all of our heart. The best fathers and mothers are first sons and daughters of the King.

So how do we pursue God?

Someone once told me, "You don't drift toward good things." So true. We drift toward laziness, overeating, and bad habits. We won't find God by drifting through life, hoping He shows up. He says in Jeremiah 29:13, *"You will seek me and you will find me when you seek me with all your heart."*

The more we pursue God, the more we grow in our relationship with Him. If you think about it, it's the same as any other relationship in our lives. My wife may be in my house every day, but if I don't pursue her, we won't have much of a relationship.

Pursuing God involves being willing to align with His ways. In the book, *The Pursuit of God*, A.W. Tozer says, "You can see God from anywhere if your mind is set to love and obey Him." So pursuit is not only an action but also an attitude. A belief system. Many of our questions in life are solved when we know who our God is. He's like a navigation system that sets the course for our lives.

This is why the Bible always talks about pursuing God with all our heart, soul, and mind—with everything we have. As we do, God reveals who we are, how we relate to Him, and how to live joyfully and purposefully. Identity, connection, healing, and purpose—all discovered in pursuing our God! And then, we can give out of what we've been given.

Pursuing God is essential to a Crazy Cool Family. Not perfection, but *pursuit*.

**son**
/sǝn/
*noun*
a boy or man in relation to his parents, a male descendant, a person closely associated with or deriving from a formative agent
*synonyms:* boy, dependent, descendant, heir, offspring

**daugh·ter**
/dôdǝr,˙dädǝr/
*noun*
a girl or woman in relation to her parents, a female descendant, a person related as if by the ties binding daughter to parent
*synonyms:* female offspring, girl, woman

*"Life isn't about how much we achieve. It's about how well we receive."*
—John Stickl, Follow the Cloud

*So in Christ Jesus you are all children of God through faith.*
—Galatians 3:26.

# Pursue God

# 3

## BELOVED SONS AND DAUGHTERS: THE WHY

You see it so often—parents with no real or meaningful connection to God, bringing their children to church or enrolling them in a Christian school because they want them to have "Christian values." Faith is not really a part of their own daily lives, but it is important for them to have their kids in a Christian atmosphere because they believe it will make their children morally good. In effect, they appreciate the value and importance of God in their children's lives, but not their own.

While something is surely better than nothing, and sometimes these children develop a relationship with God and do a great job of taking Jesus back into the home, this isn't the route God designed for the family.

Remember what was most important to Jesus? Let me give you a CCC to show you how this plays out in our family:

> GOD'S INTENT AND DESIGN IS FOR PARENTS TO LOVE THE LORD GOD WITH ALL THEIR HEARTS AND TO EMBODY THAT RELATIONSHIP BEFORE THEIR CHILDREN'S EYES.

Our family ministry is not to the children. It is directly to the parents. We absolutely believe that a huge key to a Crazy Cool Family is both parents being connected to Jesus.

If Mom and Dad are connected to Jesus, they'll do a much better job of instilling Jesus into their children's lives than any church, youth group, or Christian school.

**SUZANNE: My experience working at a Christian school proves this to be true. We have great teachers who love Jesus and love the students. We have daily Bible class, bi-monthly chapel, retreats, and mission trip opportunities. But even with this amazing Jesus-focused environment, almost always the kids with the real, authentic, strong relationship with Jesus are the ones whose parents also have a real, authentic, strong relationship with Jesus.**

## A Heart Toward God First

An encounter I had with our third daughter, Macy, can offer some clarity on the value and importance of parents having a heart towards God as they interact with their kids. This parent/teen interaction centered around our youngest, McCade. If you're around us for any length of time, you'll quickly realize he lives a charmed and carefree life. If there are perks to being the youngest, he takes full advantage. Our older kids will tell you it's because we let him get away with too much—unlike the way we parented them.

The story starts with me standing at the bottom of the stairs, calling repeatedly for McCade to get his coat and come downstairs so we could leave. What I didn't realize was that he couldn't hear me calling for him. Macy, in her room at the top of the stairs, did. After several times hearing me call to McCade, she burst out of her room and yelled at me, "He can't hear you!" She stormed into his room, grabbed his coat, and aimed him at the stairs so he could leave with me as quickly as possible. I was really bothered by the way Macy handled the situation, but I was in a hurry to leave, so I let it go for the moment.

When I got home a couple of hours later, I went to Macy's room to talk with her about the incident. Time helped. I was pretty angry when I left, but I had settled down and could approach this conversation calmly. I asked her what could possibly have made her so angry so quickly?

Macy proceeded to give me a little lecture, including many reasons that justified her behavior. When she finished, I said, "I appreciate your honesty, but if I'm honest, I don't feel any better than when I came in here. You screamed at me, and now it's all my fault." She continued in a closed fashion, defending herself.

Finally, I asked, "Macy, have I done something before this to offend you?"

Macy burst into tears, sobbing. I just waited. As she gathered herself, she began to tell me about several ways I had offended her by being selfish and arrogant. Although I could have argued she was being a little hard on me, I realized there was truth in some of what she was saying.

Now it was my turn. I could either defend myself and put our relationship right back where it was—in the ditch—or I could ask her forgiveness for my wrongdoing for having hurt her.

If I were to have listened to the flesh in that moment, I'd have argued: *I'm Dad. I'm right. You're the kid. Deal with it. Don't be disrespectful like that again.* But in that moment, I was listening for God's voice. What would He have me do? He'd advise me to humble myself, to seek forgiveness for my offenses no matter how minor they might seem to me. That's what I did, and it opened up a relationship that had been closing. Let me have Macy share from her perspective.

**MACY: Imagine yourself, sitting in your room having a peaceful morning, when all of a sudden, your father, who is already loud in general, begins yelling from the bottom of the stairs for your little brother. McCade, who is oblivious to the whole world, clearly didn't hear him.**

**My logical brain assumed my dad would climb the stairs and go to Cade's room to help him find his jacket. My mom**

hates it when we stand at the bottom of the stairs and yell for someone. She always told us to just go find them.

Yet, Dad continued to stand at the bottom of the stairs and yell, at the same volume and with the same phrase. My frustration grew and grew until I literally exploded with anger. I was so mad at him for being lazy and arrogant that I acted in haste and frustration. I yelled at him all the way down the hall and said mean things about him in my head long after he and Cade left. I was surprised my anger rose so quickly; it honestly felt like it came out of nowhere. I didn't think much of it until I heard the garage door open and my dad come into the house, making a beeline for my room.

I knew the lecture was coming. I really wasn't in the mood to hear him justify himself. I felt my emotional walls go up, and I thought, 'Just make this as short as possible.' He began to tell me how he felt and that he thought my actions were not justified. I looked him in the eyes and told him I thought he was being lazy and annoying. He wasn't pleased by what I said, but he didn't leave.

Then he asked me a question. I don't remember what he said or how he said it, but I broke. Like a dam holding water, all my heart walls came crashing down, and I started uncontrollably sobbing. I felt all the bitterness, frustration, and anger I had stored up against him come crumbling down. For the first time, I wanted to forgive him. I saw him as someone who loved me no matter what I did to him or how I acted towards him. In that moment, he was more than the guy who paid the bills and said he loved me. He was a picture of grace and mercy. He wanted to know what was going on inside my heart and why I was reacting with such anger. It felt like he came alongside me, picked me up, and gave me an empathy hug.

I completely expected he would lecture me. When he asked me questions and showed me grace, everything changed. He could have reacted harshly and with justified anger. I disrespected him horribly and deserved to be punished, but he chose to show me grace in that moment,

**come down to my level, and ask what was really going on. His kindness led to me feeling safe enough to open up and unload past offenses. His security in Jesus and his love for me in that moment gave me the courage to show him my heart and the places he had unknowingly hurt me.**

Remember the question I asked her: "Have I done something to offend you?" In that moment, rather than going into parental lecture mode and spelling out my frustrations, I allowed God to speak to me, and He showed me what was in my daughter's heart. Only the power of the Holy Spirit could break through my selfish frustration and bring healing to the situation.

This story will play out in various forms over and over in your family and ours. Are we going to assert our authority harshly and win the argument, or listen to God and win the relationship? Will the devil on one shoulder win or the voice of God on the other shoulder? I won on this occasion but have failed many times. By the power of God, I am learning how to win more and more. It illustrates one of the toughest but most important lessons we must learn as parents—in fact, if we get this one it makes everything else in our family life so much easier! We really can't emphasize it enough. Here it is in a CCC:

> PARENTS ARE BELOVED SONS AND DAUGHTERS OF GOD FIRST. OUR RELATIONSHIP WITH GOD IS OUR MOST IMPORTANT RELATIONSHIP IN OUR FAMILY.

I hate to be repetitive, but it's so important we get this. I can always use the reminder: What did Jesus say was the first and most important commandment? *"Love the Lord your God with all your heart and with all your soul and with all your mind"* (Matthew 22:37). Our first responsibility as believers is to be committed to living a life pursuing a deep relationship with God.

Why is our relationship with God the most important? Three critical reasons: (1) Power, (2) Hearing God, and (3) Example.

# Power

Raising a family is one of, if not *the*, hardest things we'll do in life. Our spouse and our kids see us every day, at our best and worst. All of our shortcomings get exposed, every button gets pushed, and every inch of our patience gets tested. We cannot expect to succeed in leading our family without the real

power of God in our lives. Trying to just gut it out, work harder, and control everything better may work for a while, but personally, I've never seen it last for a parent. At some point— more than likely at multiple points—the issues become larger than the strength we can muster. We keep trying and trying to build it and hold it together, but eventually, the house of cards falls.

*Our first responsibility as believers is to be committed to living a life pursuing a deep relationship with God.*

The answer is the power of God. The power of God working in our lives enables us to parent the way God would. And He's the best parent ever!

In that story with Macy, I was so angry with her. After all that I do for her, she was going to talk to me like that? Really? I don't deserve that. But then the power of God comes in. God reminds me of His supernatural power to have compassion on my children, just as He has compassion on me. His power allows me to forgive as I am forgiven. He reminds me of the danger of holding onto offenses. His power allows me to let it go. There's no way I can do that in my own ability. I must have the supernatural power of God.

A great example of God's power in our Bible is King David in 1 Samuel 30. Talk about a terrible day—David had just suffered the humiliation of being sent away from a battle. As he and his fighting men returned home, they discovered another enemy had raided their settlement, burned it to the ground, and taken away all their wives and children—David's two wives and children among them. To make matters worse, David's army, grieving the loss of their loved ones, became so upset with David they wanted to stone him.

I don't know about you, but that's sounding like a really bad day to me. Yet the real key is found in verse 6: *"David was greatly distressed because the men were talking of stoning him; each one was bitter in spirit because of his sons and daughters. But David found strength in the Lord his God"* (1 Samuel 30:6). The word *but* is a conjunction; it demonstrates contrast. The wheels were falling off in David's world, *but*—in sharp contrast—David found strength to face the circumstances in the Lord.

He didn't wail and complain. He didn't scold his men, telling them how ungrateful and unreasonable they were behaving... which may have hastened his stoning! Rather, in his distress, David turned to God for strength.

The rest of the story, as they say, is revealed as the chapter closes. David's men decided to follow him, and together they went and found their enemies, destroyed them, and recovered all they'd lost including their wives and children. When David found his strength in the Lord instead of cursing his circumstances, he released the power of God in and through his life. So, God gave him favor with his men, victory over his enemies, and restoration of his family. God turned a horrible day into a great one.

I think this story perfectly illustrates what can happen in our families when we turn our hearts to the Lord. Our personal and private victories release public blessings for our families. Here's how it works expressed in another CCC:

> GOD'S POWER IN OUR LIVES SHOWS US FAMILY
> RELATIONSHIPS AS HE SEES THEM.

As parents and spouses, we're going to have a lot of rough days. Maybe not quite as bad as David's day, but bad enough. The car is going to break down, the kid is going to break down, the spouse is going to break down. Only God's power allows us to see a pathway to bring life into those situations instead of adding our own breakdown to it. Let me sum that up in a CCC:

> GOD'S POWER IN OUR LIVES TURNS THE BAD
> DAYS INTO GREAT ONES.

**SUZANNE: I have a great example of how God showed me His power through His strength and joy this year. I'm always sad and a little grouchy when school starts, and the rat race of schedules, events, and agendas hit our family's time and energy. As summer was wrapping up and I was heading into my usual funk, the Lord brought to mind the Scripture: "The joy of the Lord is my strength" (Nehemiah 8:10), and He flipped the words to the strength of the Lord is my joy. He reminded me that if I try to do life in my own strength, I will be sad, grouchy, heavy laden, and burdened. But if I depend on and surrender to Him, then through His strength He will give me all the joy I need!**

And to access God's power, all we have to do is ask. Just like David did. In the heat of the moment, when the infant won't stop crying or the toddler is throwing a fit on the floor or the middle school kid withdraws or the high school student is sassy, we cry out to Jesus. He is faithful to answer our cry for help. Just read the Psalms. David cries out in the beginning, and by the end, God has met him in his unhappy place and turned his surrender into gratefulness and joy.

# Hearing God

So many family decisions are not covered in the Bible. Should I let my child spend the night over at this kid's house? Should we put our kids in public school or private school? Should I take this new job or stay at my current one? Should I encourage my kids to play sports, or does that take too much time? On and on and on it goes.

That's not even counting the many family principle

decisions that aren't covered. How long should we allow our kids to stay on their electronics? What is the right bedtime? Should I force them to eat vegetables or let them eat whatever they like? Is this a movie I should allow them to see? When is a good age for them to start dating?

The situations are endless, and unfortunately, my wisdom is not. I need the help of a wise, all-knowing God to show me the answers for my family. In a CCC:

> HEARING GOD IS NOT ONLY AVAILABLE TO US BUT IS ABSOLUTELY ESSENTIAL TO OUR EFFORTS IN CREATING A CRAZY COOL FAMILY.

Hearing God is really a key component of why we wrote this book. Imagine putting all of the issues a family will potentially face up on a wall. It would be a big wall, covered with issues. From potty training, biting, separation anxiety, sibling rivalry, and learning disorders, to bullying, grades, social situations, and electronics, and then dating, alcohol, stress, depression, eating disorders, anger, pornography, masturbation, blended families—on and on.

I'm overwhelmed already, and the wall is just getting started. We could cover that wall with more and more potential issues. Without end, really. And we don't know which ones we will face or when they will come. We don't know which kid will be affected by what. We don't know how our spouse will react. We don't know what's going to happen as we send our kids into the world. We don't know. Do you see? We don't know. But God does.

As you learn what we are showing you in this book and as you are learning to walk with God and hear His voice, you are building a framework uniquely designed for you by God to help you have the right answers to the issues as they come up. God will show you how to head off these issues before they even come up, showing you how to invest in your family relationships and teaching your kids how to hear God's voice as well.

Back to the story with Macy. My voice said, "She needs to be disciplined! She deserves it!" God's voice said, "Macy, have I done something to offend you?" My voice would have put our relationship further in disarray. God's voice created a breakthrough.

**SUZANNE: As a young parent I didn't know how to access the power of God through His voice. There were so many things we did wrong because we were caught up in what the world said or what we thought was best. You would laugh at the things we didn't allow our kids to do—play with Barbies, have sleepovers, watch Disney—the list goes on and on, and our kids still joke today about our ridiculous restrictions. We never bothered to ask our Heavenly Father His plans or ideas. As the kids got older and I couldn't keep the world away, I was forced to invite God into the raising of the children. He is faithful and wise and very willing to give His opinion on anything we ask. So instead of saying "NO," I would say "Let me pray about it." Then I would ask the Lord, "Is it a good idea for this child to spend the night at that house or watch this show or play with the latest fad toy?" And God would answer back with, "This is a great safe family, yes. This is a show you need to watch with your kids; explain why the world likes it and how it's against God's best. And those toys represent darkness, so point them to something different like Superheroes instead."**

**If you will practice asking God about the little things when they're young, when the big things come up (like if they should have a boyfriend/ girlfriend, if they should go to camp or on a mission trip, what sport to play, etc.) they will trust you to advise them well, and you will have great confidence in your guidance.**

*Our children are watching us.*

# Example

The first two relate more to our own interaction with God. But guess what, parents? Our children are watching us. They are asking the question, "What do my parents really think about God? How does the power of God play out in their lives?" A CCC for you:

---

MORE IMPORTANT THAN ANY INSTRUCTION WE WILL GIVE TO OUR CHILDREN IS THE EXAMPLE WE WILL PROVIDE OUR CHILDREN.

---

The great evangelist D. L. Moody once said, "A man ought to live so that everybody knows he is a Christian... and most of all, his family ought to know." It's true. Our words will speak to them, but our actions will speak even louder.

At this point, some people are tempted to think, "Well that ruins it for me!" Maybe you have a difficult past, failures, or addiction. Maybe you're new to the faith. Maybe dozens of reasons are spinning in your head as to why you're not the perfect Christian example. Listen to me—it doesn't matter. When I talk about your relationship with God, I'm talking about direction, not perfection.

Examples don't have to be perfect.

I have a friend who, by his own admission, is "a bull in a china shop." He is so passionate about life that many times he doesn't control his words or actions very well. If he feels something, chances are he'll express it, and with passion and fervor. He does everything he does with all he has. Needless to say, sometimes he unwittingly offends others.

For example, he may raise his voice towards his wife or kids or express something in a way he knows is not healthy. Almost always, he quickly realizes it and goes back to apologize—his actions didn't reflect his love for them.

You might think his repeated failures would make his wife or children feel alienated or distant from him. Were it not for his genuine heart for the Lord, that might be the case. But they see a husband and a father who is an imperfect man passionately pursuing a perfect God. They see God at work in his life and in theirs. They see a dad who loves God and who loves them. And all three of my friend's kids have grown up to be very healthy, spiritually alive adults.

**SUZANNE: Me first. I have to go first. I always struggle with that as a mom. It seems that the best thing to do is to serve others—especially your children first. Do you know that airplane air-mask instruction thing, the one about parents putting on your own mask before helping your children? That always stressed me out. Then I realized, if I'm not breathing, I can't help my children to breathe either.**

**That reality applies so well to my walk with the Lord. If I'm not pursuing the Lord, loving Him with my heart, words, and actions, getting filled up by His joy, strength, and wisdom, then I cannot expect the little people I am leading to be connected to the Lord in a real way. Do I pray continuously? Do I ask the Lord for directions in my daily life? Do I thank Jesus for the small stuff like a bargain at Old Navy? When Jesus is my best friend, my children see me hanging out with Him all the time, and they want to have the same best friend.**

**If we want our children to love God and love us, we must be willing to do the same. We can't live our lives indifferent towards God, call on Him only when we need Him, and expect our kids to be any different. We can't live our own lives of selfish pleasure but expect our kids to live lives of service and devotion. The best pathway for our kids to have a genuine relationship with God is for them to first see it in us.**

I asked McKenzie, our youngest daughter, her thoughts on this question: Why is it important for parents to have a relationship with God in order to connect to their child's heart?

**McKENZIE: When you, as a parent, are rooted in Jesus, it allows you to find your security in His love, not in your own**

50

strength or in the performance of your children. Jesus walked on this earth so He could relate to us in all aspects of life. Seeing Him as a perfect example, you can know this is how you're called to relate to your children. Be vulnerable, be loving, and be relatable.

One example of how to be vulnerable with your kids is to tell them your testimony. Your story is what you have to give to them and is the best way to let them know that you're not perfect.

I asked my dad his story on a long road trip. He walked me through how his parents' parenting affected him, his high school struggles, and his college choices. Then we discussed his decision to pursue Christ within our family, and this opened my eyes to the incredible man he is and how his pursuit of Christ encourages me to pursue Christ.

About a week later, my mom and I went on a date, and she told me her story. She walked me through from beginning to end, showing me how Jesus stepped into her mess continually, through different people and circumstances. When you give your children the raw truth of your walk, it allows them to see your relationship with Christ out in the open.

Your heart connection to God is extremely important because without it, there is no ceiling for your child to step on. When you share your experiences, your child doesn't have to walk through and experience the same hardships as you.

Your actions, pain, and struggles are never wasted in Christ. When you align your heart with Him, it opens the door for Him to use your testimony in your child's life.

Wisdom beyond her years. She hits on so much here. You don't have to be perfect. Key points to take away:

- Share your real faith and struggles with your kids.
- We are the ceiling our kids will walk on.
- When we align with God, He uses our life to point our children toward Him.

**MOLLIE: The biggest example from my childhood about how my parents were real and genuine was conversations about the struggles they were experiencing, struggles that affected the life we were all living. I remember my dad asking us to pray when we were younger about whether he should switch jobs, and Mom asking us to pray for her attitude and feelings about how her life was going. They were very real about their struggles and told us in a way that encouraged us to be real with each other, and most importantly with Jesus. You might worry your problems might be scary to your children, but allowing them to see that you, as parents, struggle, will help you and your faith become more real to them. Real problems lead to real conversations, which lead to genuine and strong examples of your relationship with God.**

We often ask parents, "What does your God look like to your children? Do you think they want to follow the God you show them?"

Our kids aren't attracted to a false God, or an angry God, or a critical, demanding God. But they're attracted to the God of life and love. While it would be great for them to see Dad in the Word at 6 a.m., it would even be better for Dad to be present, available, and willing to talk with his children about his relationship with God.

Our children want to know that we're succeeding and failing—hopefully, more of the former than the latter—in our relationship with God, that our relationship with God is a real and a daily part of our lives. They want to see that God is active in our lives, making a difference, making us more like Christ.

*The example of my faith is the best instruction I will ever give my child.*

My pastor always talks about "just taking your next steps with Jesus." I think that perspective really sums up what I'm trying to say here. Kids who see their parents genuinely pursuing the next steps in their relationship with God and working through the successes and failures of that relationship, are attracted to that God. Our children are much more likely to follow a God they see is real and relevant in our lives. Your life connecting with God, at a deep heart level, will encourage them to do the same.

Why is our relationship with God so important? I must have God's power for strength and wisdom, I need to hear God for direction, and the example of my faith is the best instruction I will ever give my child. I can only lead my family well through the strength of my relationship with my God. It's that simple.

**be·lov·ed**
/bəˈləvəd/
*adjective*
Greatly loved: dear to the heart
*noun*
A person who is greatly loved

*"We weren't meant to be somebody – we were meant to know Somebody."*

—*John Piper*

*Above all else, guard your heart, for everything you do flows from it.*

—*Proverbs 4:23*

# Pursue God

**God**

**Me**

# 4

---

# BELOVED SONS AND DAUGHTERS: THE HOW

You may be thinking, "I really don't understand what it means to have a relationship with God." Often in Christian circles, it's just assumed everyone knows what a relationship with God looks like. Because we're making the point that this relationship is so foundationally important, I want to take the time to explore it further.

We've told you *why* it's so important for parents to be connected to God. Now we need to consider *how* to do it. Realize that volumes of books over centuries have been written on this subject. For our purposes here, we'll have to be concise, but rest assured this chapter packs some powerful teaching on your walk with God.

When the Bible talks about a relationship with God, it talks about it as having a connection at the heart level. The Bible speaks often of the heart. Consider these passages:

*"People look at the outward appearance, but the Lord looks at the heart" (I Samuel 16:7).*

*"For where your treasure is, there your heart will be also"* (Luke 12:34). *"These people honor me with their lips, but their hearts are far from me" (Matthew 15:8).*

*"For this people's heart has become calloused; they hardly hear with their ears, and they have closed their eyes. Otherwise, they might see with their eyes, hear with their ears, understand with their hearts and turn, and I would heal them" (Matthew 13:15).*

I could list dozens of verses, but you get the point—God talks a lot about the heart. Cover to cover in the Bible, the story is the same: God desires the hearts of His people.

From Adam to Abraham to David to the disciples and beyond, God loves us and desires a relationship with His people. When this heartfelt relationship between man and God happens, you see amazing things unfold—lives changed, enemies defeated, miracles occurring—and people loving life and praising their God.

## The Heart of the Matter

What does it look like for a heart to be connected to the Lord? It comes down to two simple things.

First, we connect our hearts to God by believing in and accepting the free gift that God offers us through the sacrifice of His Son, Jesus Christ. The Bible clearly says this is not only our ticket to an eternal relationship with God in heaven, but also in this life we will have a new heart. *"Therefore, if anyone is in Christ, the new creation has come: The old has gone, the new is here" (2 Corinthians 5:17).*

Then second, a heart that is connected to the Lord increasingly perceives and understands the things of God. It seeks out the voice of the Holy Spirit and follows, no matter the cost.

What is the heart? It is the very center of your belief system. And often, the very opposite of what the world defines as the heart. When someone says, "follow your heart," what they're really saying is, "follow your feelings." But we know that following our feelings is not always the best course for us. That's because feelings are not *the heart*.

The heart is what we believe at our core. It's where real change occurs and where we must go to find the true God. Some people call it our *identity*. It's what we hold on to when we're really honest with ourselves, and not trying to be something that we're not... not trying to show off or please others.

One of the greatest books I've ever read on a heart relationship with God is *Waking the Dead* by John Eldredge. He says this about the heart: "The heart is central... The subject is addressed in the Bible more than any other topic... The Bible sees the heart as the source of all creativity, courage, and conviction. It is the source of our faith, our hope, and of course, our love. It is the 'wellspring of life' within us (Prov. 4:23), the very essence of our existence, the center of our being, the fount of our life."

So how do we grow in a heart relationship with God? We align our belief system with His truth. As we do, our feelings start to change as well. *"Take delight in the Lord, and He will give you the desires of your heart" (Psalm 37:4)*. This verse doesn't mean that if you follow God, He will give you everything you want. It means as we go deeper with God, our desires and feelings and emotions will become more in line with His desires and feelings and emotions for our lives.

Brennan Manning—no relation to me—was a pastor and a writer who pursued God with all his heart. His writings have been inspirational to me. Here are a few insights he's offered on this matter of a heart relationship with God:

"Religion is not a matter of learning how to think about God, but of actually encountering Him."

"It does us little good to memorize chapter and verse, to master the language of the Bible, if we have nothing to share in that language, no experiential knowledge of God in our lives."

"Define yourself radically as one beloved by God. This is the true self. Every other identity is illusion."

How do we encounter God? How do we experience Him? How do we trust Him? It's a lifelong journey, but as Suzanne and I thought, read, and prayed about it, God showed us four pillars we believe are foundational to a walk with God. They are: (1) Identity, (2) Hearing, (3) Healing, and (4) Purpose. Let's explore.

## Identity

In Christian circles, we talk a lot now about identity. It is a current buzzword. What it means, in essence, is this: The first thing every believer must understand is the incredible gift of God's grace.

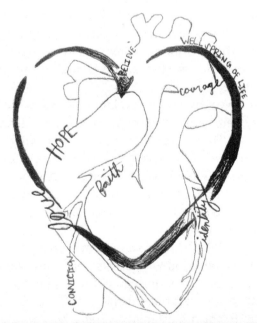

*What is the heart? It is the very center of your belief system.*

I remember many years ago a mentor friend of mine gave me a cassette tape—I told you it was many years ago—of a message on grace by a pastor named John Lynch. I thought I knew a lot about God, but Pastor Lynch told me about a God of whom I'd never heard. A God of real grace. I thought I understood grace, but I'd never really seen grace like this. In essence, Pastor Lynch's message painted a picture of God saying:

"What if I tell them who they now are? What if I take away any element of fear? What if I tell them I will always love them? That I love them right now, as much as I love my only Son?

What if I tell them there are no logs of past offenses, of how little they pray, or how often they let me down? What if I tell them they are actually righteous, right now? What if I tell them I'm crazy about them?

What if I tell them that, if I'm a Savior, they're going to heaven no matter what; it's a done deal? What if I tell them they have a new nature, that they are saints, not saved sinners? What if I tell them I actually live in them now, my love, power, and nature at their disposal? What if I tell them they don't have to put on masks? That they don't need to pretend we're close? What if they knew that when they mess up, I'll never retaliate? What if they were convinced bad circumstances aren't my way of evening the score? What if they knew the basis of our friendship isn't how little they sin, but how much they allow me to love them? What if I tell them they can hurt my heart, but I'll never hurt theirs?

What if I tell them they can open their eyes when they pray and still go to heaven? What if I tell them there is no secret agenda, no trapdoor? What if I tell them it isn't about their self-effort, but allowing me to live my life through them?"

Well, what if? Listening to that message woke me up to a different God than the one I thought I knew. The Word says, *"The Spirit you received does not make you slaves, so that you live in fear again; rather, the Spirit you received brought about your adoption to sonship. And by him we cry, 'Abba (or Daddy), Father.' The Spirit testifies with our spirit that we are God's children. Now if we are children, then we are heirs—heirs of God and co-heirs with Christ, if indeed we share in his sufferings in order that we may also share in his glory"* (Romans 8:15-17).

The believer needs to have an increasing understanding of this great truth: We are adopted sons and daughters of God, and He will never reject us! If we put our hope and trust in Him, we become children of the King forever! His love for us is eternal and never changes no matter how much we fail. Consider the story of the prodigal son in Luke 15. Jesus taught:

*"There was a man who had two sons. The younger one said to his father, 'Father, give me my share of the estate.' So he divided his property between them.*

*Not long after that, the younger son got together all he had, set off for a distant country, and there squandered his wealth in wild living. After he had spent everything, there was a severe famine in that whole country, and he began to be in need. So he went and hired himself out to a citizen of that country, who sent him to the fields to feed pigs. He longed to fill his stomach with the pods that the pigs were eating, but no one gave him anything. When he came to his senses, he said, 'How many of my father's hired servants have food to spare, and here I am starving to death! I will set out and go back to my father and say to him: Father, I have sinned against heaven and against you. I am no longer worthy to be called your son; make me like one of your hired servants.'*

*He got up and went to his father. But while he was still a long way off, his father saw him and was filled with compassion for him; he ran to his son, threw his arms around him and kissed him. The son said to him, 'Father, I have sinned against heaven and against you. I am no longer worthy to be called your son.' But the father said to his servants, 'Quick! Bring the best robe and put it on him. Put a ring on his finger and sandals on his feet. Bring the fattened calf and kill it. Let's have a feast and celebrate. For this son of mine was dead and is alive again; he was lost and is found.' So, they began to celebrate."* (Luke 15:11-24).

The grace of God is so amazing! Jesus purposefully talks about a son that has done the unthinkable. He has asked for his inheritance early, has taken it and used it on prostitutes, and is now coming back, begging just to be a servant.

There are two things about him that are significant in this story: (1) He has wronged his father greatly, and (2), he is also ready to humble himself before his father.

And look at what the father does. The father doesn't even listen to his son's story. He says, "Robe! Ring! Sandals! Food! Drink! Dancing! We are going to forgive all of the past and celebrate the return of my son!" Can you grasp this? *This* is how God loves you!

Go back to Romans 8:15-17. Does the *adopted son* now make more sense? In the story of the prodigal son, the son had given up his right to be a son. He had no rights but to be an orphan, a servant. But his father adopted him back into the family. Not as an orphan or a servant, but as a son with all the rights and privileges. Here's a CCC:

> YOU ARE NO LONGER AN ORPHAN! YOU ARE AN
> ADOPTED SON OR DAUGHTER OF THE KING!

We have wronged the Father greatly, yet His answer to us is "Robe! Ring! Sandals! Food! Drink! Dancing! Let's celebrate the humble return of my son or my daughter."

And God will love you just like that for all of eternity. His love will never decrease no matter what you do. You don't have to strive for His approval. It's already there. You no longer need to strive to become someone that is acceptable. You just live out who you already are.

Just like the father did for the prodigal son, God does with us when we humbly come to Him. He creates in us a new heart, a new identity. We have mentioned this verse before but it's worth repeating: *"The old has gone; the new is here!"* (2 Corinthians 5:17). Once we humbly come to God and accept His free gift of grace, we spend the rest of our lives not striving for His approval but living out of the new heart and new identity He gives us.

As adopted sons and daughters of the King, we don't have to act like orphans anymore. Orphans don't trust. They live in fear. They have no parents. That's the way we live outside of God.

*As adopted sons and daughters of the King, we don't have to act like orphans anymore.*

Once we are welcomed into the family—the family of the King—we now carry the full rights (and responsibilities) of that King, and we carry His power wherever we go. His incredible grace to us establishes our identity as adopted sons and daughters of the King. We can quit striving to be something that we already are and start living out of the freedom God offers us as His children of grace.

How does our new identity help us in our family?

**SUZANNE: As we deepen our identity with God, we start to see more and more of life through God's perspective. For example, instead of seeing our children as sources of irritation, we start to see them as mighty men and women of God, placed in our care to train up as Kingdom changers. When they make mistakes along the way, we see those mistakes as opportunities to turn them to the Lord. Just as our Heavenly Father does when we mess up, He uses our mistakes to draw us closer to Him… if we let Him.**

**Instead of thinking your spouse is out to get you or doesn't understand you, we start to see their hurts and wounds in the situation. This opens up a whole new mindset, showing us how the damage we do to our spouse's heart makes it difficult for him or her to respond in certain healthy ways. It leads us to pray for their heart change, instead of being frustrated by their actions.**

**When we look at our family through the lens of God, we stop thinking about what our family is not giving us or not doing correctly, and we start to be grateful for what we have. We start to realize the key to more is not demanding more but believing more and blessing them more.**

It changes everything. Jesus said, *"You will be ever hearing but never understanding; you will be ever seeing but never perceiving. For this people's heart has become calloused; they hardly hear with their ears, and they have closed their eyes. Otherwise they might see with their eyes, hear with their ears, understand with their hearts and turn, and I would heal them"* (Matthew 13:14-15).

When we understand how God sees us, we will then begin to see how He sees our family. It's not an immediate transformation, but it's a journey we take with God over time. We discover more about our own heart and our own relationship with God. As that relationship deepens, as we understand our real identity, He reveals more to us about the hearts of our family members.

# Hearing

Other than understanding grace and identity, if you asked Suzanne and me the next most important thing for the Christian parent to believe, it's about hearing God: We have a God that wants to speak with us, and we can hear God's voice clearly.

So how does the believer hear God's voice clearly? Does Scripture tell us God speaks to us? How do we know it's God? What do we have to do in order to hear well?

Our Bible—Old Testament and New—is filled with examples of God speaking directly to His people.

*"The Lord would speak to Moses face to face, as one speaks to a friend"* (Exodus 33:11).

*"The Lord said, 'Go out and stand on the mountain in the presence of the Lord, for the Lord is about to pass by.' Then a great and powerful wind tore the mountains apart and shattered the rocks before the Lord, but the Lord was not in the wind. After the wind there was an earthquake, but the Lord was not in the earthquake. After the earthquake came a fire, but the Lord was not in the fire. And after the fire came a gentle whisper"* (1 Kings 19:11-13).

*"The Spirit said to Phillip, 'Go to that chariot and stay near it'"* (Acts 8:29).

Jesus taught about hearing God with this parable in John 10. *"The one who enters by the gate is the shepherd of the sheep. The gatekeeper opens the gate for him, and the sheep listen to his voice. He calls his own sheep by name and leads them out. When he has brought out all his own, he goes on ahead of them, and his sheep follow him because they know his voice. But they will never follow a stranger; in fact, they will run away from him because they do not recognize a stranger's voice"* (John 10:2-5).

Later, He continues, *"I am the good shepherd; I know my sheep and my sheep know me—just as the Father knows me and I know the Father—and I lay down my life for the sheep. I have other sheep that are not of this sheep pen. I must bring them also. They too will listen to my voice, and there shall be one flock and one shepherd"* (John 10:14-16).

The Scripture is full of God interacting with His people.

God spoke to Moses, Elijah, and Phillip. We also see examples of God speaking to Adam, Noah, Abraham, Peter, John, Paul, and many more. Jesus says here in John 10 that we're His sheep and His sheep will "listen to my voice." The Scripture is full of God interacting with His people.

It makes sense, really, when you put it into the context of Matthew 22:37-40 as well. What was most important to Jesus? Relationship. It's kind of hard to have a relationship without talking to one another.

Our Father wants to be around us. He wants to talk to us every day, throughout our day. A CCC for you:

> WE CAN HEAR GOD'S VOICE CLEARLY
> AND KNOW IT'S GOD.

Not just every once in a while, when big decisions come up, but we can hear Him and have a relationship with Him daily, as a regular part of our life.

So how do we know it's God's voice and not our own? Suzanne has taught many, many people, including our kids, to hear the voice of God. Let Macy tell you about how she learned to hear God's voice.

**MACY: One day when I was a young teenager, Mom and I were driving home together, and I asked her how she knew what God's voice sounded like. Growing up she would always talk about what Jesus had told her or what the Holy Spirit said, and I honestly could not tell the difference between my thoughts and God's voice. I asked her and immediately began to cry. I felt ashamed for not knowing what His voice sounded like. I felt like a horrible Christian.**

**As we pulled into the garage, I remember her turning to me and asking me what I thought the voice of God should sound like. I told her I didn't know what was from God and what was from the enemy. It all sounded the same to me, and I was confused. She told me something I will never forget. She said that one way God speaks is through my thoughts, and I need to pay attention to how I'm thinking.**

**She asked me to list some positive thoughts I'd had that day. I told her I thought her outfit was pretty, Madeline's hair looked good, and I loved playing Littlest Pet Shop with Kenzie. She told me those were all amazing thoughts given to me BY GOD! She told me how God is a God of encouragement and life, and all those things were life-giving and encouraging. She said to give God credit for all good ideas and thoughts and how lots of people don't think to do that.**

**Mom proceeded to ask me to share some ugly, negative thoughts I had that day also. She reminded me that our enemy, the thief, comes only to steal and kill and destroy (John 10:10), so all those negative thoughts are from the devil. We sat there in the car for a long time talking about different thoughts and how God will never contradict the Bible, but He can speak outside of it. She told me how God gave me the Holy Spirit, He lives inside me, and constantly**

wants to talk to me. He helps me see the good in hard situations. He helps me love people who make me angry. He tells me which choice is right and wise. My mom showed me how simple it was to define God's voice without putting Him in a box. She helped me know what He sounded like in my thoughts. She encouraged me to pay attention to my thoughts for myself and how to listen for God's voice.

What a huge impact learning to hear God's voice has had on Macy's life! Her God is a God who loves her and speaks to her daily!

The Scripture gives us guardrails in hearing God's voice. God's voice will never contradict His Word. That is one reason we must get to know our Bible because it helps us to discern God's voice.

But as we've discussed, the Bible doesn't specifically address every issue we face. What school should my kids attend? Is this a discipline situation or a grace situation? Should I let my kid go over to this person's house or not? The Bible gives us direction, but God still speaks to us today to guide us in our lives.

*The Scripture calls this revelation. In Ephesians, Paul says, "I keep asking that the God of our Lord Jesus Christ, the glorious Father, may give you the Spirit of wisdom and revelation, so that you may know him better" (Ephesians 1:17).* He wants to give us a spirit of wisdom *and* a spirit of revelation.

We get wisdom from the Bible. That is God's wisdom being put on paper for us to read and receive His life-giving book that directs our lives. But we learn it not so we can know the rules. We learn it so we can understand His ways and relate to Him. Then as we face the issues of life, God's revelation can give us complete direction. We need wisdom (the study of God's Word) and revelation (hearing His voice) so we can navigate the issues of our life and our family.

So how do we know that revelation is from God and not us? If the issue is clear in Scripture, the answer is easy. But what about all these issues that aren't clearly addressed in Scripture?

How do we know we're following God then?

This leads us to answering our last question: What do we have to do to hear well? Acts 17:27 says, *"God did this so that they would seek him and perhaps reach out for him and find him, though he is not far from any one of us."* Hearing God well takes some work, but it's easier than you think because God is closer than you realize.

Here are some practical steps to help you discern God's revelation in your life:

- Pursue God through Scripture—we've covered this one already.
- Pursue God Himself—slow down, get alone with God, and let Him speak to you. As you pray, picture God in the room with you. Interact with Him as you would a trusted friend.
- Pursue God through relationships—God reveals Himself through wise counsel. One great place to start here is through your spouse. Suzanne and I will only move forward with significant decisions if we both have heard a "yes" from the Lord.

Can we get even more practical? Here are some examples of how God's voice gave us direction in our family:

**DON: For years as our family grew, God put on my heart to work closer to home. I was working in Dallas and even a normal day took 10-12 hours because of commute time. God laid the impression first and then gave me an opportunity to purchase a business that would allow me to have an office much closer to home. With that impression from God and after seeking counsel from others, we decided to purchase the business which allowed me to invest more in my family and eventually led to the birth of this ministry.**

**SUZANNE: We chose many different ways to educate our children: Mother's Day Out, homeschool, University model, full-time private school, public universities. Each year we**

would ask the Lord what was best for each child that specific year, and each year was uniquely different from the year before. Because of God's voice, I had the confidence to put my children in the best place they needed in order to be a success.

McKENZIE: I had a challenging freshman year due to my closest friends choosing to pursue other people. But it allowed me to put my foundation on Jesus and have Him be my best friend. One of the most significant truths God showed me that changed the trajectory of my life was at church camp going into my sophomore year. I felt disconnected from my community of people and realized I had to be the connector. God said "Kenz, treat people with the same love I have for you. Pursue people like I pursue you." Those few sentences from the Creator was one of the first times I understood the voice of God, and it was a critical point of understanding God's heart for people.

MACY: The summer before my junior year of high school, I sat in church and listened to our pastor talk about "creating margin" in our lives so God has room to do incredible things. I went home and thought through every area of my life. I looked at what was giving me life and what was robbing my time. I decided to stop playing sports, despite my dad's love for my softball skills, and chose to create margin for God to work in. I felt like I could breathe because there was room for new things. I started volunteering at church more and developing my gifts and heart for worship. God provided a voice/music teacher that transformed my voice and gave me the confidence to sing and to play the guitar and piano. I began to seriously pray about colleges and where God was leading me. I got into the top 10% of my class, which qualified me for automatic acceptance to Texas A&M—all because God pointed me down a different path, and I said yes. Through the process of letting go, I found God is good, and He does far more with our little than we can.

**MADELINE: I came home for Christmas Break my senior year of college with a plan. I had been dating a boy since August and knew he was the guy I was going to marry— despite the fact my family had only met him about three times, and we had only been dating for four months. The next step in my plan was convincing my parents. That was not as easy as I had thought it was going to be. Thus far in my life, we had agreed on most things. But this one was not something to be taken lightly. After Larry and I talked and talked to them about "our plan" and how convinced we were, they were still not convinced. It finally took us all taking ONE MONTH—1/4<sup>th</sup> of my whole dating relationship—to ask God and pray about it. After what felt like ages, my parents came back and said they felt peaceful about us getting married.**

God has put this ministry on our hearts for years. He provides me a way to work part-time in order to have some margin to write a book and set a vision for the ministry for the future. It's a bit of a financial risk. Is this the right timing? Do we jump out in faith? We did, and here is the book!

As with all things we practice, our ability to hear God's voice gets better over time. So, practice, practice, practice! Why would you not want the Creator of the Universe involved in your family direction? And He's free! Use Him!

# Healing

This concept is powerful in relationships. Healing our hearts is so foreign to most believers but is critical to experiencing the deep heart connection that God desires for us.

Here's the deal: As we pursue relationships inside and outside our family, people are going to hurt us. And in the past, people have already hurt us. Just like physical hurts create wounds, so do emotional hurts. They cause our hearts to be wounded. We bury these wounds, but unlike our physical wounds, the heart will not heal them in the normal process of life. They may be hidden, but they're not healed.

Do you ever wonder why some seemingly little thing makes you so angry? Why certain things irritate you to no end? Why you can't stop a certain sin no matter how hard you try? So much of our actions and reactions are generated because of belief systems based on wounded hearts. As we learn to heal our hearts, we can overcome our deepest issues of life.

After Jesus was tested by Satan in the wilderness, the Bible says, *"He went to Nazareth, where he had been brought up, and on the Sabbath day he went into the synagogue, as was his custom. He stood up to read, and the scroll of the prophet Isaiah was handed to him. Unrolling it, he found the place where it is written:*

*The Spirit of the Lord is on me,*
*Because he has anointed me*
*To proclaim good news to the poor.*
*He sent me to proclaim freedom for the prisoners*
*And recovery of sight for the blind,*
*To set the oppressed free,*
*To proclaim the year of the Lord's favor.*

*Then he rolled up the scroll, gave it back to the attendant and sat down. The eyes of everyone in the synagogue were fastened on him. He began by saying to them, 'Today this Scripture is fulfilled in your hearing'"* (Luke 4:16-21).

This is the first public statement Jesus makes, and twice He talks about freedom. Galatians says, *"It is for freedom that Christ has set us free. Stand firm, then and do not let yourselves be burdened again by a yoke of slavery"* (Galatians 5:1, 2).

So, it's possible to have the salvation of Christ, to be loved unconditionally like the prodigal son, and yet still live in spiritual slavery. What puts us in slavery? Galatians 5:1 tells us. It says, *"... do not let yourselves be burdened."* It's not God who burdens us. We let ourselves be burdened. Here it is in a CCC:

> WE CONTINUE TO BE IN SLAVERY BECAUSE WE DON'T BELIEVE THE FREEDOM THAT HAS BEEN GIVEN TO US.

Now what is freedom? It is not the right to do whatever we want. Freedom is the power to live as God wants us to live. Continuing in Galatians 5, we read, *"You, my brothers and sisters, were called to be free. But do not use your freedom to indulge the flesh; rather, serve one another humbly in love"* (Galatians 5:13).

When we use our freedom to follow God's ways, more freedom occurs. This also works in parenting, by the way (or should work this way). The better your child handles their freedom, the more freedom they should get. As we handle our freedom with God well, we move into more freedom. It creates an upward spiral in our lives.

How does exercising freedom relate to healing our hearts? When our hearts are healed, we become free. What does it look like to heal our hearts? Well, in spite of the fact that we now have the power of the Holy Spirit in our lives, there is still an enemy out there, sin is still out there, and our past is still out there. One or all of these things can cause us to be deceived. To have wrong thought processes. Wrong belief systems.

When we are saved, we are a new creature in Christ. We receive His grace, we now have the power of the Holy Spirit, and we have the ability to hear God's voice. But we must learn to walk in our new freedom. There are old ways of thinking that need to be changed.

**MOLLIE: I'm not a parent yet, but I can imagine that seeing your child hurt, either physically or emotionally, is really hard to experience. I can also imagine and have seen many of my friends with kids do this, that it's easy to beat yourself up, believe the lies that you're creating wounds or bad memories, or believe that you can't do better or be better. I've got news for you... as a kid of two sinful parents, let me tell you something you might not want to hear. You *will* wound your kids.**

**I know Mom and Dad might sound pretty perfect. They come close—but there have been times where wounds were created because of their actions. Being the oldest was great in a lot of ways, but sometimes I was a little**

neglected. That makes sense with so many kids. My parents had a hard time focusing on things going on in my life because the span of the stages each of us were living in was so large. I graduated high school three months after McCade turned one—you know, that kind of range. I was not at all prepared for college or ready to leave home, and I had no desire to apply to schools or figure out what I wanted to major in. I was basically in denial that it was time to grow up. I ended up in an orientation for transfer students because I missed all of the ones for freshmen. And I was at a college I applied to three weeks before classes started that was 15 minutes from my parents' house. It's laughable now, but the attention to preparing me for college didn't exist.

Fast forward to my junior year of college when Madeline is applying for schools, and Mom has *slightly* more time on her hands (McCade is now 4). They visit different schools and go to meetings with advisors. She decides on a school halfway through her senior year, she is signed up for all the possible freshmen activities throughout the summer, and knows exactly what she wants to major in. This continues for the rest of the kids attending college. There was a time when that lack of attention bothered me. I believed they didn't see me as deeply as they saw the other girls, that I was an afterthought, that the babies provided more joy and fun, and getting me ready for college was a chore. Lots of lies. Not at all true. But as Dad says, "This wound was an opportunity to run to Jesus." I honestly wasn't even fully aware it was there. The thoughts came here and there and got on my nerves time to time, but just by doing the things Dad said (reading the Word, having community, talking with Jesus), He began to open those parts of my heart up to a new truth. A truth that said, "I had this planned from the beginning. There was no lack of attention to detail because I am detailed in everything. You are seen, enjoyed, and valued by Me, the God of the Universe."

It took time, but that wound no longer exists. I am pumped, and I use the word pumped because I literally get giddy thinking about my sisters' experience at college. From the moment they could apply to places, to the time they moved to their dorms, and to the days where two of the three have graduated, it's all been amazing. I've shed many joyful tears alongside my parents as we've watched them grow in who Jesus wanted for them in that experience. Jesus rewrote my wound to a victory, and He can do that for the wounds you carry and the ones you worry you will make for your kids. Allow Him into those dark places. Start to release the stress of worrying you are going to create them for your kids, because their Creator will heal them in a much deeper way than you can. It's also important to note I met my husband at the college I went to. You think that was part of the much bigger plan? I think yes!

MADELINE: My parents believe in me, and they love me. I know that. Still, there have been times I've struggled to believe they are for what I want or agree with the plans God has for my life. One example is how much I love going all over the world to tell people about Jesus. I have wanted to be a missionary since I was 13. I remember heading into my senior year of college when I was offered an opportunity to help with the Syrian Refugee Crisis throughout Europe. I called my parents to hear their thoughts, and they were totally against me going. They highly discouraged it, and even said that I shouldn't go. I was astonished... and irritated. I truly felt like they were squandering the plans God had for my life. I spent time praying and seeking God on this, and as time passed, I submitted to them even though I didn't completely agree. I had a choice at that point, and, believe me, this was a tough one. I had to choose between believing my parents knew what was best for me versus believing they were trying to ruin God's plans for my life. I know that sounds dramatic, but it was the question I was asking God. Sometimes it feels hard to trust God and my parents when I truly think I know what is best for my own life. I still wrestle with this thought as I bring things up to my parents because I'm concerned that they will say, "Madeline, we don't think that's a good idea." And I will have to take my heart's questions back to God. When all is said and done, I do trust God and trust that He speaks to me through my parents, despite the realization it won't always line up with my plan.

SUZANNE: The best way I know how to heal wounds, and as you read from Mollie and Madeline above, is to realize the wound, and then with open hands and heart, give it to God to heal. Invite Him into that wounded place.

In his book, *Waking the Dead*, John Eldridge talks about bringing Jesus into the scene. Imagine the very place you were wounded, and then imagine an image of Jesus in that room.

My favorite example is when I was a little girl, I had a blanket that got left on a vacation. My grandmother wasn't fond of the blanket, so she didn't choose to get it back for me. The lie I chose to believe was that to love something and lose it is very painful, so it's better just not to love much.

That lie built so many walls in all my relationships. I kept everyone at arm's length. When I went back to the scene as a little girl and invited Jesus into the memory, He was wearing a cloak made out of my blanket, and He said, "When you love me as you loved your blanket, you will be able to love others freely." And the agreement I had made with the enemy that love was painful was broken. Now I'm overwhelmed with love for people I don't even know!

We listen to God and believe His truth over the lies that the enemy has woven into our hearts from our past. We break the agreement with the belief system that we're worthless. We start to reject the lie given to us by our parents and believe that we're amazing in God's eyes. We start to get our validation from Him and not from what our parents said about us. Our CCC:

AS WE HEAL THE WOUNDS OF OUR HEARTS, WE START TO BELIEVE DIFFERENTLY ABOUT OUR LIVES.

*Healed hearts are free to pursue relationships.*

It enables us to see ourselves more and more as the adopted son rather than the orphan. Our wounded hearts tell us we are orphans, but our healed hearts show us we are adopted sons of the King.

Healing our hearts makes such a difference in marriage and parenting. Why? Because wounded hearts get bitter and withdraw from relationships. Healed hearts are free to pursue relationships in a healthy way.

## Purpose

Our purpose in life comes out of who we are.

Here it is again: When Jesus was asked what was most important in Matthew 22, He was clear that relationships were most important, and our relationship with God was clearly the most important of all relationships. *"Love the Lord your God with all your heart and with all your soul and with all your mind. This is the first and greatest commandment"* (Matthew 22:37, 38).

Jesus was clear that His direction to have a relationship with God was our first, most important priority. As we learn our true identity, learn how to hear His voice, and learn to heal our hearts, we pursue that most important relationship well. We align our thoughts and actions with His ways.

Our primary purpose in life is to pursue God. Of that there is no doubt.

As we pursue and align ourselves with God, our purposes in life will become exceedingly clearer. People come to me all the time asking for help knowing God's will in their lives, and yet when I dig deeper, I find they are only pursuing God for the answer and not for the relationship. We pray in crisis or when we need an answer—not just to hang out with our Creator, Mentor, and Friend. Then we wonder why we can't hear God. Confusion brings so much extra effort. But God brings clarity to our purpose. I don't know about you, but when I'm unclear about my purpose, two things tend to happen: I'm stressed, (which means I'm not thinking clearly) and I do things that are not necessary (both of which are counterproductive). Let's say there's a lot going on at work. If I'm unclear about my purpose, I'm jumping around, allowing myself to be interrupted, going from task to task, not finishing anything, and I look up a few hours later with a bad taste in my mouth because I've been really busy but haven't really accomplished anything.

But let's say that I take a few minutes and map out my priorities. Then the most important project now rises to the top. I focus on that purpose and work diligently to finish it. I'm calmer because I'm only focusing on one thing and not ten. I have the capacity to finish that and maybe some other things in the same amount of time. I finish in a much better state of mind.

**SUZANNE: My role as a mom has been the number one thing that's given me purpose beyond this world. As I invest in my children, I invest in the future of our country by teaching them to be honest, hardworking citizens and honoring of authority. I invest in the nations by showing them how to love their neighbor and to be servant hearted. And most importantly, I invest in God's Kingdom plans by showing my children how to see things from His perspective and how to accept His perfect will in every situation. When I see the day to day drudge of being a mom through the clarity of God's purpose, my whole attitude and approach changes. Instead of seeing their temper tantrum as a brat not getting her way, I see it as a red flag that I have some more self-control training to do.**

Focusing on God does that for our day. We are not allowing others to dictate what we do or how we feel about it. God is in charge. He'll show us the right things to do, the right people to talk to. We move in confidence because we're confident in His love for us. We move at a slower, more in charge pace of life, yet we get more done. We have time for people and the important things of life. Our purpose is clearer, and our stress is much less.

That person focused on God operating as a parent or a spouse is an amazing person to be around. That person brings life to the family. That person doesn't get exasperated about the small things and is firm about the big things without being a jerk. That person operates out of confidence instead of fear. That person is joyful instead of being in a bad mood all the time. That person loves being around their family instead of avoiding them.

Remember, the best parents are beloved sons and daughters of God first. Here's our CCC:

> OUR STRENGTH IN PARENTING WILL COME FROM THE STRENGTH OF OUR RELATIONSHIP WITH THE FATHER.

If you believe that you have to strive for God's love, you'll make others work hard for your love. If you're a person who believes God is crazy about you, you'll have a crazy love for those around you. If you're filled with unhealed wounds and bitterness, you'll wound those around you. If you're healthy and healed, you'll bring health and healing to those around you.

I used to be so confused by two seemingly contradictory statements of Jesus. He says, "*Whoever does not take up their cross and follow me is not worthy of me*" (Matthew 10:38). Then one chapter later He says, "*My yoke is easy and my burden is light*" (Matthew 11:30). Say what? I don't think carrying a cross is a *light burden*. Do you?

Yet God is showing me how those statements flow together. When I "take up my cross" and follow God, He shows me a way of life that really is easy. As I pursue the right things and the right relationships, there's a flow to my life that's different. More peaceful, more powerful, more purposeful.

*If you believe God is crazy about you,*
*you'll have a crazy love for those around you.*

This is especially true in my family. I tell people all the time that family is the easiest thing in my life. When I pursue my family out of my identity in Christ, He shows me where to go and what to do to bring life to my family and break down any barriers that have been built. For your family, strengthening your relationship with God is the most amazing thing you can do for them.

Pursue God

God
↕
Me

# Build Relationships

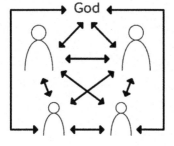

God

Create Culture

Encourage    Safe    Disciple    Unity

# SECTION TWO: BUILD RELATIONSHIPS

The strength of your family relationships will determine the strength of your family.

There are so many relationships in families: parents to God, marriage, parents to kids, kids to God, kids to kids. We've spent some time talking about parents to God. Now we're going to talk about all the others.

Of all the things I've learned about family, there are a few that have been game changers.

I began to see family through the lens of relationships. I started seeing them as real people with real hearts and minds instead of things I needed to control and motivate. I actually started to have more control over my home and became a more motivating dad. I know it sounds unconventional—this entire book is unconventional—but it works. God's ways in our family are always unconventional.

For most of us, we don't know how to do relationships. We may not have come from a family with good relationships, and we may not have a lot of them in our lives right now. We don't really love ourselves that much, so it's hard to love others and allow ourselves to be loved.

Honestly, most people give up. They try a little but then it's too hard, things get messy, and they get hurt by people they love. Over time, we replace relationships with TV or alcohol or video games or golf or work or books or music or Facebook or whatever is easier. And we begin a downward spiral toward, at best, family averageness or, at worst, family destruction.

Are you willing to fight for your family? This battle will take everything you have. You can't do it well without the power of God in your life. But if you're willing to fight and you're willing to trust God, then the positive power you'll have in your family relationships will be nothing less than astounding!

I'm so excited to share more with you!

## marriage

/mar·riage/

*noun*

the legally or formally recognized union of two people as partners in a personal relationship (historically and in some jurisdictions specifically a union between a man and a woman)

*"When you have children, your marriage is now more important, not less, because other people are counting on you."*

—Sheila Gregoire

*"A great marriage is not when the 'perfect couple' comes together. It is when an imperfect couple learns to enjoy their differences."*

—Dave Meurer

*I am my beloved's and my beloved is mine.*

—Song of Solomon 6:3

# Build Relationships

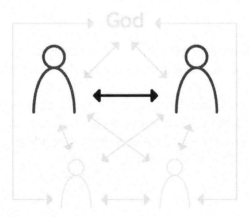

# 5

---

## MARRIAGE: FORGIVE, SERVE, APPRECIATE

Marriage. This is a tough but necessary topic to tackle in a book on creating a Crazy Cool Family.

On the one hand, we need to recognize God's best intent for marriage—one man, one woman in this fantastic, growing relationship for life. Husband and wife, holding hands, respectful of one other, great sex life, fun and memorable times, working together to build their family.

*"That is why a man leaves his father and mother and is united to his wife, and they become one flesh" (Genesis 2:24)*. We leave our families of origin to get married in hopes of something awesome. Our wedding day is a celebrated event because we're incredibly excited to start our marriage relationship and later a family that will be amazing. And that's God's plan.

On the other hand, many marriages, including many Christian marriages, don't quite turn out that way. Maybe you are a single parent. Or maybe you feel like a single parent because of a damaged relationship with your spouse. Many who will read this book will ask, "If my marriage is lost or damaged, can I still have a Crazy Cool Family?"

The answer is absolutely yes! Much of this chapter is about how to have the great marriage God intends and how marriage is a key relationship in the family. But before we go there, I want to reach out to parents that have little or no hope in their marriage. The enemy will use hopelessness in your marriage to try to hurt your relationship with God and with your kids. Certainly marriage struggles, conflicts, and failures can shake your faith and have a significant impact on your entire family.

Here's what I want to say to anyone reading this book whose marriage is in trouble or nonexistent: God is bigger than your marriage troubles!

As His adopted son or daughter, we trust in God. We can't control our spouse. We may not be able to reverse a divorce. We can't take away the hurt our marriage mistakes have caused our kids. But God can heal our hearts. And God can heal our kids' hearts. He is, after all, the *"father to the fatherless"* (Psalm 68:5). I always tell people, when you are partnering with the Creator of the Universe to raise your family, you have a great chance of winning! It is true for you.

God is bigger than your marriage troubles

We teach couples that pursuing God's best for their marriage will be a huge blessing for their family. Yes, countless times we've seen single parents experience amazing Crazy Cool Families. We've seen Crazy Cool Kids come out of families where the mom or dad are totally checked out, don't have an interest in the things of God, or are not being a loving parent.

Here's a fact: all families have issues. Because of sin, no one gets a free ride into a blissful family heaven. The major issue in your family may be a troubled marriage. But what if a family has to overcome a teenager who starts using drugs? What if a family has to overcome a parent who can't find work? What if a parent or child has a significant health disability? When we surrender to God, He can—and will—help us overcome anything! Including the difficulties of a troubled or nonexistent marriage. Jesus said so Himself: *"In this world you will have trouble. But take heart! I have overcome the world!"* (*John 16:33*).

Before we get into God's design for marriage, believe with me—declare with me—that God can overcome any marriage situation in creating your Crazy Cool Family.

There are two particular situations I want to address. Maybe you or someone you love falls into one of these categories. If so, I pray you'll be encouraged.

Single parents: What happened to get you here can be overcome by connecting relationally with God and your children. God loves you, and He has the desire and the power to overcome the lack of a second parent in creating your Crazy Cool Family. As you connect more deeply with God, you'll grow in wisdom, strength, courage, and hope to more deeply connect your children with God and with yourself.

Married to a checked-out spouse/parent: Perhaps you're pursuing God, but your spouse isn't. It can feel as if your spouse is growing away from you and the family. Maybe he or she is only there physically, having checked-out spiritually and emotionally. God loves you and your spouse, and He will honor *your* pursuit of Him. God can overcome a checked-out parent in creating your Crazy Cool Family. A powerful way to invest in this kind of relationship is to pray cease-lessly for your spouse, to serve them with no expectations, and to love them like Jesus does with acceptance and

*The parent who serves a difficult spouse is an awesome example of the love of Jesus to their children.*

encouragement. You may be thinking, "Impossible!" True—in and of your own strength, you'll certainly grow weary—but as you depend more on your Heavenly Father, He will give you the desire to pray, the ability to serve, and the abundant love to share. I've seen it happen! The parent who serves a difficult spouse is an awesome example of the love of Jesus to their children.

Be encouraged! We've seen God do this sort of thing over and over again. Sometimes it even baffles me: How does this kid love Jesus so much when the mom left for another man? How does this mom hold her family together when all the dad can think about is money and career success? How can these kids love Jesus when there's such conflict in the home?

God is bigger. Believe it.

Declare it.

I think we can all agree that it would certainly be better to have a strong marriage relationship to build our family upon. Just like it's so much easier for the family if all our kids love Jesus, family is certainly easier and smoother with two parents who love Jesus, love each other, and work together to create a Crazy Cool Family. How do we make that happen?

We'll share a few key points Suzanne and I have discovered about marriage, but let me point out this isn't a book on marriage. It's a book on a framework for your family. There's a wealth of great and very specific material available on how to have an excellent Christian marriage. Since marriage is so very important to the family, I encourage you to pursue much more than I can offer you here. We've listed a few of our favorite resources for you in the appendices. Check them out.

Why is marriage is a driving force in the family? Several reasons. Let me spell out a few of the most important ones.

## Strong Marriages Provide Stability in the Home

My parents have been married over sixty years. When I was growing up, I never had so much as a thought that they might get a divorce. That doesn't mean they had a perfect relationship—remember we all have issues—but they never gave me a reason to think their marriage wouldn't last a lifetime.

As I look back at the impact their strong, stable marriage had on my life, God has shown me how that provided a rock-solid stability in my life I still carry with me. Just like we carry our parent wounds with us into adulthood, we carry their strengths as well. The stability in my parents' marriage gave me stability that I've carried into my family.

**SUZANNE: The story of my family is completely different. I had amazing parents, but they had a very dysfunctional marriage. My dad traveled all the time. He was never home to build a family with my mom, my sister, and me. Honestly, I was scared of him for the first decade of my life. He was a stranger. He wasn't an angry man at all, but he was an introvert and very hard to connect with. I think my mom, my sister, and I were always trying to win his approval, and he was clueless on how to give it. My parents never fought or had any kind of conflict that I ever witnessed, but even as a child I could tell they were not connected. I remember when my friend's parents got a divorce in the 6th grade; I thought my parents will probably do that someday. And I predicted correctly. For my 18th birthday, my mom moved out. They tried for about a year to reconnect, but too many years had passed, too many wounds had been suffered, and there wasn't enough Jesus in their lives. So, as Don brought an example of a stable relationship to our marriage, I brought all the things we should not do if our marriage was to succeed. The main thing I learned from my parents' failed relationship is that to make a marriage successful, both spouses choose to love Jesus most, and then out of the overflow of the love from the Father they can love each other.**

How do we make our marriages stable? And can we go beyond stable? How about great? Fulfilling? Fun? I'll give you three words that will make your marriage awesome: *forgive, serve,* and *appreciate.*

Suzanne and I have been better parents than we have marriage partners. Our marriage has never gotten in the danger stage, but we've struggled to have a marriage that's really fulfilling. For sure, having seven kids has taken up a lot of time we could have spent with each other, but it's more than that.

We're both very independent, and we have different personalities. She likes being at home, and I love to go places. She is hands-on, and I'm a delegator. She's more sensitive and emotional, while I'm more even keeled.

What's important is we share a strong faith in Christ and we really want our marriage to be strong. I love to tell people we are living proof that marriage can work between two people who are very different.

**SUZANNE: Don and I are both the baby of our families—in other words, we can be really bratty—so we've had to really learn how to forgive, serve, and appreciate each other. Marriage is probably the hardest thing I've ever done in my life, and I have a great husband—so that must mean marriage is one of the most difficult relationships God puts us in. The mom role is easy because I'm the boss, in control, what I say goes until I start handing over the control to them. And even then, I'm still pretty much in charge. I get to form, mold, and build little people to be a lot like me. Not so much with the husband. He comes fully equipped with all his own ideas, agendas, and control issues. And just like I don't want to give up my stuff, neither does he. To be very honest with you, what caused our marriage to not be fulfilling is the time we neglected to invest in it. We're great parents because we have chosen to invest LOTS of time in training, raising, and releasing our children. So, while doing all that, we let our marriage coast for a couple decades. But as Don said above, our strong faith has kept us on the same page with the importance of our marriage. We're looking forward to being empty nesters, when we**

can invest more time in each other. **Writing this book together has been a wonderful eye-opening experience that God has used to knit us together on a whole new level, and it has given us many opportunities to forgive, serve, and appreciate each other! Those three words have been real difference-makers for us.**

## Marriage is About Forgiveness

Our life verse for our marriage is Ephesians 4:32, *"Be kind and compassionate to one another, forgiving each other, just as in Christ God forgave you."*

In a marriage, we have to choose to forgive every time. Actually, that same concept works for any relationship. Remember when Peter asked Jesus how many times to forgive his brother? Peter thought seven times was a lot, but Jesus essentially told Peter to forgive every time, all the time.

Forgiveness opens up a relationship. Conversely, the lack of forgiveness closes a relationship. It rejects the other person and pushes them away. One day the rejected person decides, "I don't want to be rejected any more. I don't want a relationship where forgiveness is withheld." The ultimate end to the marriage may be an affair, but the start was the wedge created in the relationship by unforgiveness.

The enemy also uses our own unforgiveness to build up bitterness in our own hearts. I have seen it happen so many times. The walls of unforgiveness on both sides are built up so slowly so the strength of the dividing wall is deceptive. The distance is so gradual, and then one day the couple looks at each other and feels very little. Maybe nothing.

**SUZANNE: Ephesians 4:26 says, *"In your anger do not sin: Do not let the sun go down while you are still angry."* Can I confess something? This was my issue as a young bride. I'd go to bed pretending to not to be angry, saying "Everything is fine," in hopes that in the morning it would be fine. And it never was. I would practice conversations in my head all day that should have been said the night**

before. I gave the enemy an open door to torment me all day long. And when you add up years of that, you get a distant marriage.

So now we have some code phrases we use when one of us starts shutting down. In bed, before we go to sleep, we say, "How do you feel about me right now?" or "Do you like me?" It's not a threatening question, and it opens the door to conversations about offenses. But most importantly, it closes the door to the enemy, preventing him from building a case against your spouse all night and being distant and cool all day. Forgiveness is a game changer in the spiritual realm that translates into the physical realm of relationships, and I believe we totally underestimate its power.

It's funny. The kids notice it more than the parents do sometimes. They sense the distance, and it can cause them to fear that their parents may get a divorce. How can it not? They see divorce happening all around them.

When they see their parents being cool toward each other—not as in Crazy Cool, but cool as in distant—it shakes their foundation. They may not even know what's wrong, but the sense of marriage instability puts a burden on them. And it doesn't matter how well you think you're faking it; they see the lack of eye contact, hear the cool tone, and notice how you're not touching or joking or laughing. Your kids are very observant and very smart.

That's one reason we talk about our marriage conflicts and resolutions with our kids. Not all the time—and we certainly don't share everything—but we want our kids to know that our marriage is strong and healthy and full of forgiveness. We want to be real with them about our marriage, and make sure they know we're not hiding things from them.

Just go through the New Testament and search the word *forgive* to see what all God has to say about forgiveness. You'll see God believes forgiveness is incredibly powerful in all relationships. Since marriage is our most important relationship, maybe we should try it there.

# Marriage is About Servanthood

In his letter to the Philippians, Paul introduces Jesus as the greatest servant ever. Then he says we should be servant-minded like Jesus. *"Do nothing out of selfish ambition or vain conceit. Rather, in humility, value others above yourselves, not looking to your own interests but each of you to the interest of others"* (Philippians 2:3).

He doesn't stop there. He goes on to spell it out. *"In your relationships with one another, have the same mindset as Christ Jesus: Who, being in very nature God, did not regard equality with God something to be used to his own advantage; rather, he made himself nothing by taking the very nature of a servant, being made in human likeness. And being found in appearance as a man, he humbled himself by becoming obedient to death—even death on a cross!"* (Philippians 2:5-8).

Wow! If anyone had a right to use His power, it was Jesus. But He didn't. He made Himself nothing. Did you catch that? *Nothing.* Zilch. Zippo. Nada. Here's our CCC:

> WE FOLLOW THE EXAMPLE OF JESUS BY TAKING ON THE ROLE OF SERVANT IN OUR MARRIAGE.

He could have made Himself something. In fact, the disciples were begging Him to make Himself a physical king and take over the Roman Empire. He had armies of angels at His disposal. Yet, He went to the cross.

Please don't miss that this passage instructs us to apply servant-mindedness "in your relationships." It doesn't say to practice this "in your relationships where everything is going well" or "in your relationships where everything is easy." It says, "in your relationships." Period. In other words, *in all your relationships.* And who is the most important relationship after your connection to God? You've got it—your spouse.

**MOLLIE: When my husband Damian and I started planning our wedding, there was a lot of conversation about what**

message we wanted our ceremony to speak and what vision we wanted our guests to experience while attending. Aside from wanting our guests to know we love Texas, country music, and Mexican food, we wanted them to recognize the very basic truth that marriage is an earthly picture, a human way of comprehending in our pea-sized brains, the beauty and depth of the gospel. That Jesus came to earth, died on the cross, and rose again so the church could be His Bride. Revelation 19:7 says, *"Let us rejoice and be glad and give him glory! For the wedding of the Lamb has come, and his bride has made herself ready."*

Now, this is easy to communicate on your wedding day. It's THE BEST DAY EVER, right? But what does it look like within marriage? That's a different story, but a story that can be created, formed, and communicated if your marriage is rooted in servanthood. Damian likes to call our fights "difficult dialogues." This fits his personality perfectly. He is positive and a goal-achiever. He likes to see things as something spurring you on to something greater. I, on the other hand, am blunt, see things as black and white, and call it like it is. A fight is a fight. Call an argument what it is, "difficult dialogue" is far too kind of a name for what actually happens. But one evening on a lovely date-night, when a discussion turned into what I would call an argument, he explained his meaning behind a difficult dialogue. As a lover of Jesus, a member of the church, we're called to be like Christ, to be imitators of God, as it says in Ephesians 5. As we work on our relationship with God, talk to Him, explore what our journey with Him looks like, we start to become more like Him; and in return, others around us experience knowing God. John 13:35 reads, *"By this everyone will know that you are my disciples, if you love one another."*

This is no different in a marriage. In fact, it's an even greater opportunity because your spouse sees it all, and they know you at your worst and see you at your best. To Damian's point—as my husband, he is called to love me like Christ, and in doing so he's making himself more like Jesus.

**To him, a difficult dialogue only sharpens his faith and our relationship, like the Proverb says, *"As iron sharpens iron, so one man sharpens another."* In a difficult dialogue, we're exploring together as a couple what it looks like to respond in love, to respond in growth, and to respond in forgiveness. Out of all this comes the idea of servanthood.**

Servanthood is difficult in a marriage for many reasons. I've seen a lot of marriages in my life. I've never seen one that's easy. Once I heard a speaker say the reason fairytales end after the prince finds his princess is because marriage is no fairytale. To that we would all add a hearty, "AMEN!"

The issues start with the fact that it is a man and a woman. I don't care what the politically-correct agenda tries to throw at us—men and women are very different. We think differently, and we love and receive love differently. All men and women are not the same. These differences necessitate the need for servanthood.

**SUZANNE: Don's and my marriage took a turn for the better when I stopped trying to turn him into a hairy woman. I'd get so frustrated that he didn't think the way I did. As soon as I let go of the expectation that he should be exactly like me and started embracing the fact that he's not—this world doesn't need two of me, one is more than enough— I began to see our differences as an asset to our marriage. Let me tell you, the ol' marriage started to change. Don felt more accepted, and I wasn't constantly frustrated with him.**

It does indeed seem, for the most part, like opposites attract. This is one of those questions I want to ask God when I get to heaven—Was this by design? If we're so smart, why do we pick marriage partners who are very different from ourselves? If we waited and picked later in life, would we pick more similar mates? I don't think so. I think God wired us this way because He knows it's best for us not to have similar people around us but different people. It stretches us, makes us learn, and draws us to God.

*What if marriage is designed to make us holy?*

**SUZANNE: I completely agree.** These opposite qualities are exactly what God prescribes so we will need, depend on, and surrender and cling to Him as we try to relate to our spouse. In his book, *Sacred Marriage*, author Gary Thomas asks the question, "What if marriage is designed to make us holy?" That's a powerful paradigm shift in thinking about our differences. My experience is when something comes up that I don't like or agree with, I go to the emotions of frustration or irritation. However, if I filter those feelings through an invitation of Jesus coming and believing this very situation will make me more holy, then it's not as bad a deal at all. It's actually a great deal. Kind of like when your freezer breaks and everything thaws so you're forced to throw a big party or make dinner to share with all your neighbors. Seems bad, but it's really a whole different kind of good that you would never have experienced. Your situation created opportunities to bless and grow. So, I challenge you... start asking yourself and God the question: How can the differences between my spouse and I make me holy? And sit back and see what God can do when you allow Him to change your perspective.

Finally, we have the whole sin issue. We're not only different, but we both bring baggage into the relationship that impacts our marriage. Our insecurities, weaknesses, fears—all of these and more—can make us selfish, withdrawn, moody, untrusting, and spiteful. God's solution? Servanthood.

Put your spouse ahead of yourself. All the time. It means we take the kid to practice instead of sitting on the couch. It means we unload the dishwasher instead of going to bed. It means we respond with kindness even when they're grouchy. It means we listen to God's voice when we want to be selfish.

**SUZANNE: My love language is *Acts of Service*, so one would think I have this part down in my marriage. Wrong. The language that we speak is not usually the same one that our spouse speaks, as is true with Don and me. His love language is *Quality Time*. So, while I'm running around the house like a crazy woman cooking him food, ironing his clothes, and cleaning up so the house looks nice, he wants me to sit down and have a quality conversation with him, which is the last thing I want to do. The lesson I've learned on serving my spouse is to ask myself, "What does he need, and how does he want to be served?" That's the key. Not so much how *I* want to serve him. It's so like God to turn it**

| Love Language | What to Communicate | Actions to Take | What to Avoid |
|---|---|---|---|
| Words of Affirmation | Compliments Encouraging Words Affirmations | Write the person an encouraging note. Praise the person publically. | Criticism |
| Quality Time | Intentional, one-on-one time. Not interrupting. | Make time in your schedule to spend with this person. | Long periods spent apart. More time spent with others. |
| Receiving Gifts | Positive, fact-oriented information. | Put thought and time into a gift. Give gifts on ANY occasion. | Forgetting special days or reasons for celebrating. |
| Acts of Service | Use action words like, "I can," "I will," or "What can I do?" | Help with chores, repairs, tasks. Any act of kindness or helpfulness. | Ignoring partner's requests while helping others. |
| Physical Touch | Use non-verbal communication. Verbal should be in "word pictures." | Touches Hugs Cuddles Holding Hands | Physical neglect or abuse. |

upside down so that we must depend on and ask Him how best to serve our spouse. We cannot do it in our own understanding or strength. We must see our spouse through God's eyes, and only then can we serve him how he best needs to be served. Take a look at the chart on the previous page (information gathered from *The Five Love Languages* by Dr. Gary Smalley). How did God wire you? Your spouse? How can you best love and serve each other?

It sounds crazy, but then so does God sending a baby to earth over 2,000 years ago to save the world. Just like Jesus gave it all for us, we have to be willing to give it all up for our marriage. But what if it doesn't work? You have faith. But what if my spouse hurts me? You go to God for healing. But what if my spouse keeps being selfish? You keep serving like Jesus.

We believe in what Paul says in Philippians 2. We serve, even when it doesn't feel like we're going to win. We consider others above ourselves, even when it seems like our spouse is being selfish. Have the same mindset as Christ Jesus. Sounds crazy, doesn't it?

The pathway to a great marriage relationship is servanthood.

Look what this servant-mindedness accomplished in Jesus: *"Therefore, God exalted him to the highest place and gave him the name that is above every name, that at the name of Jesus every knee should bow, in heaven and on earth and under the earth, and every tongue acknowledge that Jesus Christ is Lord, to the glory of God the Father"* (Philippians 2:9-11). Jesus' servant attitude and actions resulted in God giving Him the "highest place." He wants to do the same for your marriage relationship.

The pathway to a great marriage relationship is servanthood. Day in, day out. Serve and love and encourage your spouse, and let God take care of your needs and desires.

## Appreciate, Not Improve

Honestly, I'm surprised Suzanne didn't leave me during the first ten years of marriage. Don't get me wrong, I loved my wife, but there was a difference in the way I loved her and thought of her then versus now. In my mind, I was ahead of her spiritually, and I felt she needed my help to be a better Christian and a better mom.

I tried so many ways to help her. I designed organizational systems for her, tried to help her study her Bible better, told her frequently how she could improve things at home. I really was trying to help. I had her best interests at heart, but it communicated to her that she needed to improve to be accepted by me.

Somewhere around the ten-year marriage mark, the Lord opened my eyes to what an amazing woman I married and how I needed to stop trying to change her. She was so relational, so intuitive, and so discerning. She radiated God's love to others.

My view of her changed, and then our relationship started to change. I started to appreciate her more and tried to improve her less. As I changed, she felt better about herself and—spouses, this is huge—she started to trust me more. Suzanne started to look at me as a husband who loved her right where she was, rather than the husband who was always trying to help her get better.

I can see the wheels spinning in your head right now. "I thought I was supposed to help my spouse improve. Isn't that part of my role?"

Yes, but let me flip that thinking a little. What if instead of telling our spouse how they can improve their lives, what if we spent our time:

- Praying for our spouse?
- Creating an environment for your spouse to be his or her best?
- Telling them how awesome they are?

It's my testimony that this is the real pathway toward building the best marriage. Maybe your spouse invites your

97

helpful criticism and wants you to speak improvement into their lives, but in my experience with my marriage and counseling others, I rarely see it happen that way. The husbands who adore their wives, and vice versa, are almost always the ones with a great marriage. Here's a great CCC:

> WE SHOULD TRY TO IMPROVE OUR SPOUSE
> LESS AND APPRECIATE THEM MORE.

**SUZANNE: I, too, spent the first decade of our marriage trying to enforce my improvements on Don. Externally: get braces, contact lenses, grow hair out. Emotionally: don't get angry, don't even allow your frustrations to show. Spiritually: listen to God better, feel His presence, lead our family. The list went on and on as time went by, and I continued to shut my husband down until God opened my eyes to a pathway of appreciation. He started filling my heart with gratefulness for the very handsome blue-eyed man I'd married. He showed me what a consistent pillar of strength and wise, mighty man of God Don was underneath all my improvements. My thoughts and actions toward Don changed, and that created new life in our relationship. Ladies, I challenge you to do an experiment: watch your husband's countenance after you praise and encourage them. His shoulders will go back, and his head will be held high in confidence like a mighty lion ready to conquer the world. I underestimated the power of appreciation in my young marriage. Hopefully you'll learn from my mistakes. Make an intentional choice to stop trying to improve your man and start speaking life through appreciation of him.**

Appreciate means "to raise in value." It also means "to place a high estimate on." We married our spouses for good reason. There are qualities in them that we admire. Our marriage changes when we see our spouse as a person of value rather than someone who needs to improve to meet our standards. We speak life into them and build them up rather than tear them down. We see them differently and they see themselves differently.

Let me finish where we started in this chapter. A single mom or dad can absolutely create a Crazy Cool Family. A family can overcome a checked-out spouse. The other parent can still have great relationships with the kids and can still lead the kids to Jesus.

But a family with marriage issues is not God's best. God wants the two to become one flesh. We believe that any two Christians who want their marriage to work and are willing to give of themselves to it can create a unified marriage. When a marriage is stable and servant-oriented and has two people who really appreciate each other, the marriage becomes the crossbeam of the family.

## awe·some

/ôsəm/

*adjective*

extremely impressive or daunting; inspiring great admiration

*synonyms:* amazing, magnificent, wonderful

*informal*

extremely good; excellent

*Awesome as in:* "Your kids are awesome!"

*"Identities and destinies are both formed and destroyed by declarations made by parents."*

—Patricia Bootsma, Raising Burning Hearts

*Children are a heritage from the Lord, offspring a reward from him.*

—Psalm 127:3

# Build Relationships

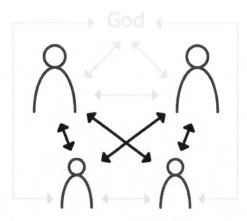

# 6

---

## PURSUING THE AWESOMENESS
## IN YOUR KID

As the kids get older and go to college and get married, it gets harder and harder to get everyone together in our family. One chance was over the summer in Gulf Shores, Alabama. All eleven of us—Suzanne and me, seven kids and two sons-in-law—stayed together at a house we rented there. It was timely. I was right in the middle of writing this chapter on how we develop relationships with our children.

One night I looked around the room as everyone was watching a movie and was so grateful that Suzanne and I have great relationships—I'm not kidding, great relationships—with every one of our kids. The girls, the boys. Younger. Older. We have Crazy Cool connections with all our kids. And now even our sons-in-law.

I thought to myself, "How did this happen? What can I share with parents to help them have the Crazy Cool relationships with their kids that God has given us with ours?"

This whole book is about relationships. Throughout it, we'll give you many practical ways to connect with your kids, so this chapter will be very short. As Suzanne often tells me when I'm speaking and repeat myself three times to make sure everyone has the point, "Honey, we need to honor their time."

But don't let the brevity diminish the importance. What I'm about to tell you about connecting with your kids totally changed my family. Let's start with a CCC:

> YOUR KIDS SHOULD BELIEVE YOU THINK THEY ARE AMAZING AND WORTH PURSUING!

I could end the chapter right here. If I could declare this statement over you and implant it into your heart so you would practice it without fail, you would dramatically increase your chances of having a kid who loves you, loves their family, and, most of all, loves Jesus.

Why is this so important? Because God designed a child's relationship to the parent to be the most influential relationship in their lives. What we think of them is a big, big part of what they think of themselves.

When a child believes in his heart that his parents think he is amazing and worth pursuing, that child has an easier time transferring that identity to God.

Look at what God did with His Son. As Jesus was about to start His ministry, He went to be baptized by John the Baptist. Matthew 3:16-17 says, *"As soon as Jesus was baptized, he went up out of the water. At that moment heaven was opened and he saw the Spirit of God descending like a dove and alighting on him. And a voice from heaven said, 'This is my Son, whom I love; with him I am well pleased.'"*

**SUZANNE: Before we get into how to communicate acceptance to our kids, I want to point out my favorite part of this passage. God is announcing Jesus to the world. It's a giant billboard saying, "PAY ATTENTION WORLD! This is my Son! He is amazing, and WE have a plan to change the world." Parents, we get to do that with our kids, too! When we encourage our kids in front of people or talk highly of**

them to others, it grows courage and confidence in them. So many times, when I tell a parent how amazing their child is, they come back with something the kid does wrong. For example, I'll say, "Your child took such initiative to clean up after our meeting." And the parent will say, "I wish they would do that in their room or our kitchen." What would it look like if we believed our children will do great things and be great, and IF we agreed with people when they notice our kids in a good way? What would it look like if we screamed from the mountaintops so everyone could hear how incredible we think our kids are? "I'm WELL PLEASED with this daughter/son of mine!" We would build a beautiful foundation for our kids.

God communicates three things to Jesus we need to communicate daily to our kids:

1. WE CLAIM YOU.
2. WE LOVE YOU.
3. WE ARE PLEASED WITH YOU.

*We claim you.* God declares to everyone, "This is my Son!" Our children need to know beyond doubt we are proud to have them in our family. We claim them. We're honored that God has chosen us to be their parents. We're excited we get to do life with them.

*We love you.* Our kids need to know our love never stops. Never. Romans 8:38 says, *"For I am convinced that neither death nor life, neither angels nor demons, neither the present nor the future, nor any powers, neither height nor depth, nor anything else in all creation, will be able to separate us from the love of God that is in Christ Jesus our Lord."*

Our kids need to see this same type of love from us. The kind that says, "No matter what happens, there's nothing you can do that will stop us from loving you with all our hearts. If you push us away, we won't push back. If you run, we'll wait for you to return. We'll believe in you and work for your good as long as we are alive."

*We are pleased with you.* This one may be the hardest, but it is oh, so critical. Actually, I shouldn't use the word "critical" in this statement because being critical is our greatest issue.

If God told me He would give parents one gift—and only one—I'd ask Him to give them the gift of seeing their children as God sees Jesus and as He sees their children.

You wouldn't be so scared anymore about how they will turn out. You would see your role is to draw out what is already there rather than try to control their bad behavior. You would see their amazingness and talk to them about that rather than what they were doing wrong.

*Ask God for the gift of seeing your children as He sees them.*

And they wouldn't be scared of you anymore. They wouldn't be waiting for the hammer to come down because of every little mistake. They wouldn't feel like they never could quite measure up. Quite the contrary. Their hearts would be filled up because their parents think they're awesome!

Honestly, Suzanne and I believe the number one thing we've done as parents to help our kids turn out well is to learn to love our kids in this way. We've never done consistent discipline well. We're not very good at checking their grades or making sure they've done their homework. We rarely feel like we are on top of our parenting game when it comes to keeping up with all the *stuff* parenting requires.

But we do really focus on the same thing God communicated to Jesus at the baptism. We want our kids to know without a doubt, "This is my child, whom I love; with him (or her) I am well pleased."

As we instill over time—over and over again, day after day—this belief they're amazing and worth pursuing, they believe they're valuable! Kids who believe they're valuable are confident. They're able to receive love. They don't want to do things that will hurt themselves (Why would they hurt something valuable?).

What's really cool is a kid who believes they're loved and valuable and amazing and worth pursuing is very receptive to a God who loves them just like his parents do. We'll do a whole chapter coming up on how to connect your kid to Jesus, but let's say here that as parents we don't need to beat our kids down so they'll feel like a sinner and turn to Jesus. Trust me. The world will do enough of that for them.

When our children feel from us the same love God feels for them, they'll be much more open to receive God's love. We can still know we're sinners and yet also believe that we're worth

*When our children feel from us the same love God feels for them, they'll be much more open to receive God's love.*

pursuing by the Creator of the universe!

Suzanne and I were talking to a good friend of ours who knows our kids well, knows about the book and the key points we were trying to communicate to parents. This friend is a youth pastor who works with many young people and their parents. He said this to us: "When I look at your family, what separates your kids from others I meet is two things: Their relationship to God and their relationship to you. You guys pursue relationship with your kids at such a high level. I think it gives them incredible confidence that their parents think so highly of them that they are worth pursuing."

Here's the cool part: Anyone can do what we do! Anyone can pursue their kids! Anyone can believe in their kids! Anyone can be grateful for their kids as a gift from God! Anyone can tell their kids how awesome they are!

Now, it does take some effort. Not just physical effort, but belief effort. It's actually much easier to yell at them and try to control their lives. It really doesn't take belief to do that. It's much harder to be the encouraging, believing parent who sees the best in their kids and works to draw it out! To be that parent, we have to do things like give our fears to God, let go of some things that annoy us, and be willing to not be in control all the time. Remember, our kids are not ours—they're on loan from the Creator for a short time.

As we teach parents to pursue their kids, some people say we're enabling "helicopter parents." What's a helicopter parent? A parent who thinks their child can do no wrong and is overly involved in the life of the child, "hovering" over them to make sure everything is just perfect.

As you'll see in the rest of this book, our helicopter crashed a long time ago. It is very possible to believe in your kids, be engaged relationally, while still allowing them to make mistakes.

The best way I can describe it is to think of a one-year-old learning to walk. We enjoy and take pleasure in their mistakes as they get up and fall back down. Why? Because we believe through their efforts and mistakes, the child is going to learn to walk. In the same way, when we see the child as fearfully and wonderfully made by God and believe God is going to win their heart, we see their mistakes totally differently, as a normal part of the life of an amazing child!

It really is a totally different way of thinking about interacting with our kids. But it works!

**MADELINE: When I was growing up, my parents had PLENTY to do. My main love language was Quality Time. I love being with people! I could spend every minute of every day with people and around people and go to bed feeling filled up and alive. This meant there was never "too much" time my parents could spend with me. The fact of the matter was they had six other kids, a full-time job, church small groups, their own friends, bills to pay, and about 10,000 other things also needing their time and attention. What I needed as a kid was intentional pursuit from my mom and dad to believe I was important and valuable to them. One of the ways my dad would do this**

was by taking me on smoothie dates or simply just inviting me along with him on his errands. I would feel so included in his life. I would get in his car and just talk and talk and talk all about all my life updates. Some of my favorite memories with Dad were the times he just included me in his normal life. It didn't take much effort, but it helped make me feel amazing and worth pursuing!

MADDOX: I think being coached by my dad in sports helped build my relationship and respect for him. We spent so much time in the car going to events, and he always asked me questions about my life. Spending time together is the way to get to know somebody. My dad is not a far-off, distant figure. He is up-close and personal, and he annoyingly wants to be in my life. I'm not like Madeline at all; I'm much more of an introvert. I don't like it when Dad makes me go on errands with him, but I'm glad my parents always make it a point to spend time with me.

I lead a group of men from our church, and we regularly meet in the barn behind my house. I have a marker board out there I write on when I'm out there thinking about stuff. One day God gave me this phrase for my life: "You have what it takes!" It really spoke to me, so I wrote it on my board.

One of the dads in the group saw it and started speaking it to his three-year-old son every night when he put him to bed. Three years old, and the dad is speaking life to him. He's totally bought into the program.

He took the statement and added his own wording to it. Then he came back a few weeks later and told me every time he leaves for work, his son now says to him the statement God gave to him: "Dad, you have what it takes! You're the man!" Can you just see the dad and son building each other up?

Then it gets better. Later he sent me an encouraging email that said this:

"Sometimes I have trouble connecting with my six-year-old daughter. I would rather play hoops than Barbies. We had been talking about making our kids feel amazing. One evening right before our group, she was playing Barbies, and my son really wanted me to play hoops. I told him I was playing with his sister right then, and we'd have to play later."

"After I played with my daughter, she asked if she could walk me out to the car. As I backed out of the driveway, I rolled down the window to wave bye and she yells out, 'You have what it takes, Dad! You're the guy! You're bold!' I hadn't said that to her nearly as much as to my son. But when I invested in her and made her feel amazing, that statement just came out of her!"

That dad is training up Crazy Cool Kids! He's pursuing his relationship with God, he's investing in his kids, and he's showing and telling them they're amazing and worth pursuing!

Any parent can say this about their kid. Why do I know that? Because every child was created by God. And God doesn't make junk! He's created every child special. He's created every child in His own perfect way.

Psalm 139:13-15 says, *"For you created my inmost being; you knit me together in my mother's womb. I praise you because I am fearfully and wonderfully made; your works are wonderful, I KNOW THAT FULL WELL* (emphasis mine). *My frame was not hidden from you when I was made in the secret place, when I was woven together in the depths of the earth."*

We can say to our kids without hesitation, "You're made in the image of God! You're created exactly how He intended, and He's inviting you into His purposes for your life! Go, mighty warrior!"

Can I get you to buy in? Will you go after your son or daughter like God did with Jesus? Will you ask God to show you how to be a mom

*Believe that they are amazing, communicate it all the time, and then watch it happen right before your eyes!*

or dad who shows their kids they're amazing and worth pursuing? Believe that they are amazing, communicate it all the time, and then watch it happen right before your eyes!

"This is my son (or daughter), whom I love; with him (or her) I am well pleased!"

## a·live

/əˈlīv/

*adjective*

living, not dead; in existence, in use; active, animated; having interest or meaning

*synonyms:* ongoing, vital, spirited

## dis·ci·ple

/dəˈsīpəl/

*noun*

a follower or student of a teacher; a personal follower of Jesus during his life

*verb*

to train, educate, teach

*"The greatest legacy one can pass on to one's children and grandchildren is not money or other material things accumulated in one's life, but rather a legacy of character and faith."*

—Billy Graham

*Pour out your heart like water before the face of the Lord. Lift your hands toward him for the life of your young children.*

—Lamentations 2:19

# Build Relationships

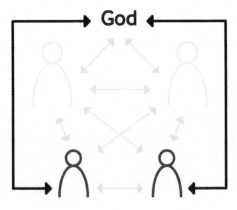

# 7

## THE EASIEST KIDS TO RAISE ARE KIDS WHO LOVE JESUS

Such an important truth, it's both the title of this chapter and our next CCC:

THE EASIEST KIDS TO RAISE ARE KIDS WHO LOVE JESUS!

For the Christian parent, there's no greater joy than knowing your child loves the Lord. As they grow up and develop their own relationship with God, you're seeing the answer to years of your prayers coming to life. You're seeing the evidence, the fruit of the Spirit in their lives. They love others, they're full of life, they share your values and beliefs, and you have a connection with them that transcends the physical realm.

On the other hand, there's no greater burden for the Christian parent than a child who's distancing from God as they mature. There's an abiding fear—this child might forever forsake the salvation that God offers. The lack of shared values can cause division and discord in the family. Believing parents worry about the choices their unbelieving child makes as they struggle to find meaning and purpose in life apart from God and faith. Perhaps as you read these words you can relate.

This leads to a key question: How do we lead our kids to a strong relationship with God?

Let's get real. As parents, we're terrified that whatever bad conduct our teenagers engage in while they're under our roof will only multiply when they move away from our care. We secretly believe every instance of disobedient behavior is a strong indication their heart is much closer to the darkness of the world than the light of the gospel. So, we lecture. We punish. We try to control. And we get frustrated.

We worry. We worry when we're alone. We share those worries with our spouse. We want to share our worry with peers, with other parents, but we're nervous—what if our kid is the worst one or other families aren't having these problems? In reality, they're thinking the same thing. That's why when you ask, "How are things?" the standard neighborly answer is, "Good."

But let's ask real questions: What do we do with these little beings God put into our care? How do we show them the Father without driving them away from Him? How do we help them find God for themselves while still protecting them? It's confusing. There's great tension between protection and trust, safety and freedom.

It's easy to forget in parenting that your child is an actual person with their own heart, feelings, emotions, desires, and dreams, finding their own beliefs. We need to parent accordingly.

Do you remember playing with toys as a kid? Chances are— whether you exhibited moments of spoiled-brat behavior yourself or *you had this friend*—you've experienced a child throwing a fit in anger because it didn't do exactly what he or she wanted. I'd suggest we sometimes parent like that, throwing a fit because he or she underperforms our wishes and wants. We lecture, we punish, we want to control.

But they're not toys. Just like you and me, our kids are

beings, made in the image and likeness of God, and entrusted to us to raise, nurture, and guide. Think of it this way: our children have the same questions about God that we do; they're searching for the same answers; they're facing the same spiritual challenges. A CCC for you:

---

OUR CHILDREN ARE GOING ON THEIR OWN JOURNEY
TO FIND THEIR RELATIONSHIP WITH GOD.

---

They're coming to their own conclusions about Him. This process is unfolding whether we, as parents, like it or not. Our children must—and will—make their own choice where God is concerned. We cannot make the choice for them.

Jesus commanded, *"Therefore go and make disciples of all nations, baptizing them in the name of the Father and of the Son and of the Holy Spirit" (Matthew 28:19).* How do we obey that command in our home to make disciples of our children? Fortunately, God's Word gives us a lot of direction in helping our children develop a dynamic relationship with the Lord.

As I was writing this chapter, I believe God showed me from Scripture an acronym that encompasses five critical elements of the environment you want to create as parents to help bring your children along in their faith. Please know, I'm not a big fan of employing clever acronyms or witty slogans for every parenting issue that comes along, but I think this one really works. It takes something lofty—like leading your kid to Christ—and makes it something easy to remember.

The acronym is ALIVE. We make God ALIVE for our kids! ALIVE stands for these critical elements:

**A**sk – We ask God fervently for our kids to connect with God's heart.
**L**ive – We live out God's example daily.
**I**mpress – We impress God's Word into their hearts.
**V**alidate – We validate their hearts by encouraging their faith questions.
**E**xperience – We create and encourage faith experiences.

# Ask

In her book, *The Power of a Praying Parent*, Stormy Omartian says, "Being a perfect parent doesn't matter. Being a praying parent does."

So often overlooked, prayer really is the single most important thing you can do to help your child into the kingdom of God. I cannot tell you how many times Suzanne and I have had a frustrated parent come to us and tell us their child isn't interested in the things of God even though they, as parents, try to talk about it with the child all the time. My advice? Leave the child alone about God for a while and pray like crazy for a breakthrough. Think about it—no one likes a pushy salesperson, and especially not where the most important decision one will ever make in their lives is concerned. Beating your kids over the head with Jesus won't work. Talking with God about your kids does. Prayer is the most effective tool you have to usher God's voice into the life of your child.

As a praying parent, you have the ear of God.

God establishes authority structures in this life with purpose and design. He honors them and works through them. *"Let everyone be subject to the governing authorities, for there is no authority except that which God has established. The authorities that exist have been established by God. Consequently, whoever rebels against the authority is rebelling against what God has instituted, and those who do so will bring judgment on themselves"* (Romans 13:1-2).

He established the family as His primary and most important authority structure. As a praying parent, you have the ear of God. He gives you the authority of heaven to open up your child's heart.

Now, here's where it gets a little tricky. Notice in the second verse it says, *"whoever rebels against the authority is rebelling against what God has instituted, and those who do so will bring judgment on themselves."* As you fervently pray for your son or daughter and they're not in line with God's direction, you may see God allow some unfortunate events in your kid's life. There may be some pretty tough consequences for decisions they make and actions they take. You may see their hearts really become troubled as they wrestle with issues that may have been awakened by your prayers. Realize these consequences are designed to make them see that life on their own, away from God, is not best. You'll want to rescue them and save them from the hurt, but the pain may be the catalyst to bring them to a new perspective and a different path. This is where you trust—your Father knows best.

Pray as if your children's lives depend on it. Think of it like this: How would you pray for your child's physical health if, God forbid, she were in a life-threatening accident and doctors weren't sure she'd make it? You'd cry out to the Lord with all you have, with every ounce of fervor you could muster. Cry out to God where your child's spiritual life is concerned in the same way!

The Bible says that King David was a man after God's heart. He is a great example in Scripture for how to have a relationship with God. We see so often in David that he didn't just pray—he cried out to God. Look at these verses:

*"In my distress, I called to the Lord; I cried to my God for help"* (Psalms 18:6).

*"To you, Lord, I called; to the Lord I cried for mercy"* (Psalm 30:8).

*"Come and hear, all you who fear God; let me tell you what he has done for me. I cried out to him with my mouth; His praise was on my tongue. If I had cherished sin in my heart, the Lord would not have listened; but God has surely listened and has heard my prayer. Praise be to God, who has not rejected my prayer or withheld his love from me"* (Psalm 66:16-20).

In this passage, David gives an absolute clinic on how to pray. He cries out to the Lord, and he praises Him. He comes to

God with his heart as pure as he can. He humbles himself before the Lord, giving up his rights to sin. Through his cries to the Lord, David sees God do great things. God heard and answered his prayers.

Crying out is valuable as we pray for our kids. Another aspect of praying is to pray continually.

**SUZANNE: 1 Thessalonians 5:17 says to "pray continually." I interpret this not as a prayer thrown up as I'm falling asleep, but more like a prayer that starts when I get out of bed, when I see the child first thing in the morning (Thank you, Lord, for this sweet child), as I cook them food (Lord, help this food bless their bodies and feed their soul because it's made with love), and continues as I do their laundry (Clothe them with Your Spirit today and wash them clean), help with homework (Have them grow in Your wisdom), and go to their sporting events (Protect them from the ways of this world). The whole time, all the time, I'm bringing them before the Father, crying out on their behalf for His love, favor, peace, strength, and supernatural power in their lives. Here's another CCC:**

> CRAZY COOL PARENTS UNDERSTAND THEIR BEST CHANCE TO LEAD THEIR CHILDREN TO THE LORD IS THROUGH FERVENT AND CONSISTENT PRAYER.

How serious are you about your child's relationship with the Lord? Are you trying to lecture them into the kingdom, trying to sell them on your faith under your own power? Or are you crying out to the Lord for Him to soften your child's heart, watching to see where God is going to work? Are you continually putting your child before the Lord for their relationship with Him?

## Live

Children will follow your example of a genuine relationship with the Lord much easier than they'll follow a theory, a lecture, or a sales pitch. And referring back to God's intent and design for the family and its authority structure, that's exactly what He has in mind.

Here's a vitally important CCC we shared earlier, which bears repeating:

---

**THE EXAMPLE WE SET FOR OUR CHILDREN IS MORE IMPORTANT THAN ANY INSTRUCTION WE WILL GIVE THEM.**

---

Look at this passage of Scripture: *"These are the commands, decrees and laws the Lord your God directed me to teach you to observe in the land that you are crossing the Jordan to possess, so that you, your children and their children after them may fear the Lord your God as long as you live by keeping all his decrees and commands that I give you, and so that you may enjoy long life"* (Deuteronomy 6:1-2).

God communicated these instructions to His people so their *children and their children after them may fear the Lord.*

Here are the instructions: *"Love the Lord your God with all your heart and with all your soul and with all your strength. These commandments that I give you today are to be on your hearts. Impress them on your children. Talk about them when you sit at home and when you walk along the road, when you lie down and when you get up. Tie them as symbols on your hands and bind them on your foreheads. Write them on the doorframes of your houses and on your gates"* (Deuteronomy 6:5-9).

We will look at this passage again, but for the moment notice the emphasis to parents—*you, parent, you love the Lord your God with all your heart, soul, and strength.* Then you, parent, take what God is doing in your life with these commandments, and you, parent, talk about it in the normal course of your day. For us, this is when you sit at the kitchen table, when you go to your kid's sporting events, when you tuck your kids into bed at night, and when you're taking your kids to school in the morning.

Now do you see why we spent so much time on your being a son or daughter of God, prioritizing your relationship with

God as the very foundation for your kids coming to Christ?

Notice the instruction unfolds, *"These commandments that I give you today are to be on your hearts. Impress them on your children."* And be sure—when God's commands are written on your heart, that will speak volumes to your kids.

When we talk about parents being an example, I know it can bring up worries, regrets, and even guilt. We're flawed and fallen human beings. You may be thinking you've not been a very solid or consistent example of having a Christian walk before your children. This can make you reluctant to talk to your kids about spiritual matters, as if your failures impeach you.

*When God's commands are written on your heart,*
*that will speak volumes to your kids.*

But let me challenge that thinking—those thoughts are nonsense and a great tool of deception in the hands of the enemy. He's the accuser. He's the one who would have you paralyzed in worry, regret, and guilt. Your Heavenly Father cherishes you—like you cherish your kids.

We're tempted to try to do an end run around our failures, trying to cover them up, and avoid transparency with our family. Trust me, your kids will see through your hypocrisy. If you're trying to be someone or something you're not, if you're trying to put on a religious show for them, your testimony is dead in the water. But where you talk about your relationship with God in humility and authenticity—where they see a real relationship with the Lord with real repentance and reconciliation—they have a front-row seat to the genuine article. They love you. They desire a real relationship with a real you. Be real.

MOLLIE: I love it that my parents were real with me in showing me their relationship with God. Your own dynamic relationship with God allows your children to see Him in your lives. Just pause for a minute and think about that. When was the last time you told your son or daughter about something God did in your life? I don't care how old they are. If I could pick one thing from this book to tell you, if I had one sentence to tell you how to be an effective and amazing parent, it would be to tell your children how God shows up in your life.

There is not a time in my life when I don't remember my parents being open with us about what God was doing in their lives. My dad is super smart. He has a master's degree in accounting and is a very hard worker. He did the whole corporate America thing while being involved in church, and then felt the Lord was calling him to be on staff at the church. As you can imagine, corporate America pays better than the Lord's people do. I remember my dad coming home and asking us to pray for this decision. He asked me, as a nine-year-old, and Madeline, as a five-year-old, to pray God would reveal answers to him about whether he should make this move. He let us in on what God was doing in his life.

We're older now, but whenever I go home to visit, without fail, and no matter how long I'm home for—two hours or two days—someone in my house asks me what God is doing in my life. Then they proceed to tell me what God is doing in theirs. You know why this is a daily conversation at the Mannings'? Because my parents started those conversations before we could even talk.

You may think something big has had to happen in order to talk about what God did. Sometimes He does show up that way. But more often it's, "Mom, I was so nervous about my speech today, and I said a quick prayer before I got up and my nerves went away." I literally remember saying to my dad on the way home from a game once, "I prayed my free throws would go in, and they both did!" Those are answers to prayer. But we've had stories of speaking in tongues, people getting healed, Jesus revealing sin in our lives, and so much more.

Think about it like this: When you're excited about something, you tell the people you love, and in return, they become excited for you and with you. When God is working in your life, you should be excited to let your children know. As they see God moving in your life, they'll store it away in their developing, curious brains, expecting God is going to move for them too.

Hearing those recollections of Mollie's takes me back. Suzanne and I didn't do anything dramatic. We didn't hold seminars at the house or have 5 a.m. Bible studies—full disclosure, I may have tried a few of those, but they didn't work very well. We just decided that our children were going to be involved in our relationship with Jesus. As God spoke to us and we wrestled with God over issues, we talked about it with our family. It wasn't formal. It was just a part of our daily lives. And it worked.

**SUZANNE: As Mollie mentioned, a great question to use in your home is, "What is God doing in your life?" It opens up beautiful conversation. It keeps the focus on God, and it builds faith. I love sharing things God is doing in my life because it reminds me that He is real, and He loves me enough to be involved in the details of my life. But I really love hearing what God is doing in each of my children's lives. That makes me love the Lord even more because His ways are so much better than my ways. What He's doing in my children's lives blesses me doubly.**

Someone once said, "Children are great imitators, so give them something great to imitate." The best we can give them to imitate is a humble, genuine walk with Jesus, full of mistakes and victories.

## Impress

So many parents look to their church, youth group, or Christian school to teach their kids about the things of God. Those are great supplements, but if they are your only method of putting God's Word into your children, you abdicate your primary role as a parent. Pastors, youth ministers, and teachers will tell you, they cannot be as effective as you—their role is to come alongside and supplement what's already happening in the home. Here's a CCC:

> PARENTS ARE TO BE THE PRIMARY TEACHERS OF GOD'S WORD FOR OUR CHILDREN.

It's not rocket science. Parents don't have to be Bible scholars to bring God into the home. It's really as easy as those first two points we've discussed—pray and let your kids see your walk. Talk with your family about what God is doing in your life. Let me give you a few practical ways you might open those lines of conversation.

For starters, Suzanne mentioned the value of the question, "What is God doing in your life?" Lead by example. What's something God is working on in your life right now? How has Scripture impacted your life recently? What verse has God put on your heart to help you take your next step in your faith? Share that with your family. Ask them to pray with you about it. Then ask what God is working on in their lives. Ask how you can pray for them. Your kids might not have anything to share at first. And that's fine. They'll appreciate that you were willing and wanted to listen to them. And just like that, the conversations are underway.

*What is God doing in your life?*

Does your church or school send home Bible memory verses? If so, memorize them with your children and talk about how they could obey that verse. Don't turn it into a competition or lecture your child if they don't get every word right. Enjoy it. Make it fun. Remember the goal is to get everyone comfortable talking about the things of God.

McCade had to memorize Ephesians 4:29 for his class at the school he attends: *"Do not let any unwholesome talk come out of your mouths, but only what is helpful for building others up according to their needs, that it may benefit those who listen."*

As I was helping him memorize it, I said, "I love that verse! That is so valuable." As we worked to memorize, it was helpful to break the verse into parts. With each part, I told him how the Scripture spoke to me—that I only need to say helpful things, not hurtful; that I need to say things that are not my own agenda but are helpful according to others' needs.

I asked him how he could use that verse at school as he interacted with his classmates. Instead of just going through the motions to get the verse done so we could both go watch TV, it was a great opportunity to take God's Word and implant it in both of our hearts.

**MADELINE: As a little girl, I remember Dad coming to my room at night before we went to bed and teaching us Psalm 1. As a kid, he had memorized it in a chant/song form, so he would "rap" it with us at bedtime. It actually was a lot of fun, not boring or forced at all. I remember it to this day because of his sharing it with us every night. He only did it for a short season, but it was enough to get it embedded into my mind and heart.**

**MOLLIE: Recently I went on a mission trip to Thailand with my husband, Michael, and Macy. One of the days there, we helped to sort books for a free Christian bookstore in Bangkok. I looked up at one point, and Michael and Macy were running toward me laughing with a book in their hands. They had found the kid's Bible Dad read us every night growing up. Talk about nostalgia. There, in the middle of nowhere in Thailand, with my little brother and sister, we sat and read Bible stories we didn't even have to**

read because we knew them by heart. The story of David, the King after God's heart; of Esther, the brave queen; of Noah and the big flood and the promise of the rainbow; of the Good Samaritan; and Zacchaeus, the wee little man. There were the Bible stories that created the foundation of our knowledge of the Bible. Dad read to us out of that book far more nights than I can remember. All of us, even when I was 12 and the boys were babies, would sit and listen. Usually by then I was doing the bedtime reading, but that's beside the point. We loved it, and we learned so much from the simple three-page stories.

MACY: I was trying to remember what we used to do on Saturdays. I know when we got older, we played a lot of sports. But I remember when we were super young, after we had breakfast on Saturday mornings, Dad would teach us Bible verses. He made up songs and clapped in a beat, the beat depending on the type of verse. Happy, sad, instructional, each had its own beat. We'd sit on the floor, and he would stand there saying the verse with the beat; we'd repeat it, over and over again. At some point he would stop and talk about the words, what they meant, what we thought God was saying, and then we'd go back to the beat, clapping and saying the verses. I learned a dozen Psalms this way. I still can't say them to this day without at least tapping my foot to keep the beat. I don't ever remember being bored or annoyed. That's what we did on Saturday morning. I remember thinking it was pretty cool to have all that Bible knowledge in my head, and in retrospect it was pretty cool of my dad to spend his weekend imparting biblical knowledge to his kids and bringing it down to our level. It might have taken us weeks to learn one portion, but we did it all the time, and lots of it.

MADDOX: My family goes to church basically every Sunday. When I was younger, I hated it because I didn't like children's church. Children's church was too simple, and regular church just felt like a man talking to me about things I didn't need to know. But when we'd go out to lunch after church, my parents and all my sisters would talk about the sermon, and I wanted to be a part of the conversation. So, the next few Sundays I started paying attention to what the pastor had to say. And I realized what he was saying was valuable because he gave me things to focus on and try to fix. Then I had things to add to the talks during lunch, too.

Are you going to church as a family? Listen to the sermon. Take a few notes. Ask your family how God spoke to them through the message. How did the pastor use a Scripture to make a point? Be willing to share with them what you learned and where God spoke to your heart. Conversation—not a sermon rewind. Your goal is to welcome, foster, and encourage spiritual dialogue.

Suzanne has done a great job of putting Scripture throughout our home. All over the house in the décor, there are various Scriptures. On the wall in the living room, on the counter in the kitchen, even in the bathroom. Especially in the bathroom! Our kids were talking the other day about how they had memorized 10-15 verses of Scripture but had no idea how they memorized them until they remembered that it was on a wall somewhere in our home.

**SUZANNE: I take Deuteronomy 6:9, "... write them on the doorframes of your houses and on your gates," very seriously. To me, that means everywhere. I have pillows, plaques, and pictures of verses all over my house. Any excuse to redecorate, right? But to be honest with you, the places that were the most valuable in driving the Scripture in was next to the children's bedside and their bathroom, right by the toilet. They see it several times a day!**

**When I teach Bible classes, I tell my students to hang their Scripture memory verses by their toilets and mirrors. When we subconsciously look at something several times, it goes deep into our subconscious and settles in our heart.**

The Bible is a relationship book, not a rule book. It's full of stories of imperfect people following a God who loves them and wants the best for them. We see their hopes, their disappointments, their discouragements, their victories, and their failures. Sharing these stories with age-appropriate books and videos are a great way to get God's Word into them—and you.

For your three-year-old, it may be a simple Bible story book with pictures that tell the story of David and Goliath and Noah. For the 12-year-old, it may be watching *The Bible Project* on YouTube, or watching The Bible miniseries, or just reading a Bible story with them.

*The Bible is a relationship book, not a rule book.*

Scripture memory can be hard, but it's very effective in putting God's Word into your kids. This year, our church had a theme that came from a passage in Ephesians. They encouraged us to memorize this passage, so Suzanne and I challenged everyone in the family to do it. Not only was it a great way to memorize Scripture, but we also got to show our kids an example of how God speaks to us through our local church.

Don't make it hard. God wants Scripture to be a regular part of our lives. Be creative. If you're having trouble, ask the Lord for ways to bring out Scripture. He loves His Word; so chances are if you ask Him, He'll be pretty open to giving you some ideas.

**SUZANNE: I'm terrible at knowing where a verse is located in the Bible. I'm just not good with numbers. A quick confession: I don't know any of my kids' cell numbers. But not knowing the Scripture references doesn't stop me from constantly sharing God's Word in conversations with my kids. I quote verses all the time as if I thought of them... and technically, if the Holy Spirit inside me thought**

the words, then so did I, right? And I use Bible stories and characters as living examples. Like when my kids are fighting a battle with something, I'll say, "Remember how David took on Goliath, a giant, because he knew he had God on his side? Well you have God on your side just like David did." When we incorporate the language of the Bible into our everyday conversations, it makes the Bible relevant and alive to our kids.

Remember what we said about hearing God's voice. Scripture is one way God speaks to us. The more our kids understand and believe His Word, the more they're going to follow His voice.

## Validate

News flash: It's quite okay for your children to go on a journey as they learn about Jesus. As they mature, it's natural for them to have questions about who God is, whether He's real, and how they interact with Him. We should be more concerned if they don't ask questions, not when they do.

You want to encourage your children to ask questions about their faith. Their questions give us opportunities to explore faith with them in a safe environment. As they ask and learn, instead of being lectured and shut down, they start to own their faith. God becomes a friend they can trust.

Think of the way Jesus brought faith out in His disciples. One great example is found in Matthew's gospel. When Jesus walked on the water to meet His disciples, Peter asked, "Lord, if it is you, tell me to come to you on the water" (Matthew 14:28). You know what happened next. Peter got out of the boat and started to sink. Did Jesus lecture Peter? No. He reached out His hand, steadied him, and asked, "Why did you doubt?" Here's a great CCC for you:

FAITH GROWS IN QUESTIONS AND DIES IN LECTURES.

It's natural for our kids to ask questions about their faith. It's natural for them to want to explore their surroundings. I can relate. I explore anything that's interesting to me. Whenever I go to a new place, the first thing I want to do is to go check it out. I look up the history of the place, check out things to do, look at the map to get the lay of the land.

There's no quicker way to kill communication with your children than to shut down their questions by giving them pat religious answers or trying to manipulate with fear that they're going to hell if they doubt. You'll make them feel their questions are stupid. They'll stop asking. And you'll have done immense damage.

**SUZANNE: My experience has been the big faith questions really start coming when kids are in middle school. Just the other day, Maddox, in 8ᵗʰ grade, asked, "Did God create sin?" That led to, "Is God a puppet master?" Which led to, "Why did He even create us?" Which led to, "Are there other beings He created we don't know about?" And wow, was it hard not to drill him with all my answers and opinions and the realizations God has given me on those very topics.**

**I had to practice my self-control and contain my know-it-all attitude, which is hard for the faith-filled teacher in me to do. I asked him questions based on Scriptures so he could discover the answers for himself. Now, of course, I shared my opinion, too. But it was only after he shared where his thoughts had led him. It's important they ask the questions, and it's very important they find the answers that point them back to God.**

If you want to lead your kids to Jesus, if you want their faith to become real, and if you want yours to grow in the process, then invite their questions. "Dad, if God is good then why did my friend's parents get a divorce? Doesn't God love them? Didn't we pray for them?"

What a great opportunity for you as a parent. Engage. "That's a great question, Son. What do you think the answer is?" And to be sure, when you don't know the answer to one of their questions—and rest assured there will be questions you cannot answer—asking their thoughts and their opinion is a great tactic. It says, "Let's give this some thought." And many times, you'll need that time to collect your own thoughts! And then talk about it. Don't be scared. Have faith. Remember our first letter stands for "Ask"? We are praying like crazy for our child to have a real relationship with God and believing that relationship is going to happen. Here's an answer to that prayer unfolding. Here's a great opportunity for you to explore matters of faith together, with your child. Bonus! We both get to learn.

Our job as a parent is to help lead our children to their own faith. Questions help validate their journey.

## Experience

Look for opportunities to get your children involved in things that can lead them to the Lord. Suzanne calls this tactic *creating opportunities for spiritual encounters*. Here's a CCC:

> PARENTS CREATE SPIRITUAL ENCOUNTERS TO HELP THEIR KIDS EXPERIENCE JESUS FIRSTHAND.

**SUZANNE: Imagine life's events being weighed on a scale with the world on one side and the things of God on the other. The world is diligent to fill up its side of the scale with life's good and bad experiences, like a 100 on a spelling test, a home run in kick ball, someone cutting us in line, a birthday party, or the childhood experience of a lifetime— Disneyworld. Get the picture: the world side of the scale is full! Our responsibility as parents is to balance the scale or, even better, to make the spiritual side of the scale weigh the most.**

**What are some good opportunities for spiritual encounters?**

**Yearly: summer camp, Vacation Bible School (VBS) at your local church, or maybe family camp.**

Monthly: worship concerts, conferences, or a pre-teen or teen retreat.

Weekly: church services, a Bible study, youth group, movie night with family or friends that has a spiritual emphasis.

Daily: worship music in the car on the way to school, prayer or Scripture before they go to bed, or conversations about what God is doing in their lives (we call these God stories).

An amazing spiritual experience is to serve the Kingdom together either at church, a local mission, helping a neighbor, or on a mission trip. There is something very powerful about leaving our comfort zone and serving God on missions with people we love the most.

Many of us have a story of the Lord speaking to us in our teenage years, through a youth camp or retreat, an evangelistic event, or something else we attended that was out of the norm. These can be life-changing events for your kids. McKenzie shares of her experience at a summer youth camp.

McKENZIE: I've only attended two camps in my life, and they both changed me in profound ways. In 2013, my church sent a large group of students on a three-day adventure to seek Jesus. I'd been at the same church for my entire life, but I didn't have a group of friends within the student ministry. So, for three days, my mission was to pursue everyone I could; I didn't want anyone to feel the lack of friendship like I had experienced. I remember walking down a very long trail to get to the worship place and talking to anyone on the path. This opened my eyes to the importance of pursuit. By the end of the trip, I'd met and knew by name about half of everyone at the camp, continually trying to love everyone. On the last night, God showed me in the song, "Oh How He Loves," that He loved me and thanked me for loving His people. As I looked out at the crowd, my eyes filled with tears—I was overwhelmed with His love.

The next year at camp, He opened my eyes to how I was a sinner and how every worship time, devotion, and conversation brought me into a closer relationship with Him.

Church camp is incredibly important because the relationships you form there will continue through every week, Wednesday services, and Sunday mornings. When a family is rooted in a church, the pressure of friends at school understanding you and accepting you is no longer a necessity, but a bonus. After I pursued God's people in 2013, He blessed me with 10 to 15 new, extremely close friends. Parents, release your fears of not constantly holding your child's hand because some of the most successful parenting is in the times of release.

*Parents, relax your grip. Some of the most successful parenting is in the times of release.*

Macy shares a story of how valuable it was to serve in VBS at our church for years as a family and the spiritual growth and life lessons she gained.

**MACY: VBS caused crazy spiritual growth for me and my siblings as we grew up. We were given the chance to serve and not be served. As a family, we chose to serve in the church which taught me to see the local church as a place to give, not take. During the week before VBS, we spent countless hours at the church painting, cutting, and stapling decorations. I walked into each VBS with ownership of my church because I helped put it all together. As a family, we made it "mandatory" to go and, once we were old enough, serve in VBS. It was part of our family's identity to serve in the church, even when we didn't feel like it. One summer, I came back from Uganda, and the next morning I reported to serve on the VBS worship team. I felt jet-lagged and**

overwhelmed from everything I'd seen while on mission, and I didn't feel like leading little kids in worship. But I committed to my church, and VBS was the chance to hold true to my word. God was so faithful because it was the best of all the VBS's I had led.

VBS holds a special place in my heart because it's where I experienced Jesus consistently during the sporadic summertime. It was a safe place and a launching pad for me in my relationship with God. I loved serving alongside my family and how we made it a priority. It gave the local church a deep place in my heart, and to this day I believe the local church is the beloved bride of Christ. VBS gave me a foundation that fostered my faith for the rest of my life. And it gave me the confidence and practice I needed to lead worship in the season of life I'm in now.

Here's a story from Madeline about her trip to China with her dad.

MADELINE: God put missions on my heart when I was about 13. I love going all over the world to tell people about Jesus! I love the adventure of travel and the joy of doing what Jesus says in the Great Commission (Mathew 28:18-20). One of the most significant things my family did for me was encouraging my passion for spreading the name of Jesus to the nations. Mission trips weren't the most common thing for them (at the time), but they put their concerns and fears aside and encouraged me to listen to what God was saying to me. Before my sophomore year of high school, my dad helped organize a trip for him and me to go to China with a group from our church. In my mind, this was the best possible thing. Being able to do something I love with my dad felt like I was winning the lottery. For my dad to take the time out of his busy life to go with me felt like he cared about me in such a deep way. Not to mention that he also realized that the need to share Jesus with the whole world was bigger than himself, his time, and his money. My favorite part of that trip was

**getting to travel around China and preach the good news of Jesus. Since then, I have had the opportunity to go around the world telling more and more people about Jesus. But the one that will always hold a significant place in my life is that trip to China my sophomore year, because I got to go with my biggest fan, my dad. Join your kids in their passions. It's a great way to help them experience God in a big way.**

Is there a camp, retreat, youth activity, or mission trip where your child might encounter the Lord? Gently, not forcefully, encourage your child down these paths. You never know what will be the catalyst, but making efforts toward involving your child in spiritually-rich environments and with spiritually-minded people will enhance their opportunity to connect with God.

We make Jesus ALIVE for our kids. *Ask* through prayer for their connection to God! *Live* and be an example of God's love for them! *Impress* His great Word into their daily lives! *Validate* their personal faith with your encouragement, and create spiritual *experiences* for them to balance out the ways of the world. That sounds a lot like God's instruction to us in Deuteronomy 6, doesn't it? *"These commandments that I give you today are to be on your hearts. Impress them on your children. Talk about them when you sit at home and when you walk along the road, when you lie down and when you get up"* (Deuteronomy 6:6-7).

**friend**

/frend/

*noun*

a person whom one knows and with whom one has a bond of mutual affection

*synonym:* companion, confidant, familiar, playmate, workmate

*"There's no other love like the love for a brother. There's no other love like the love from a brother."*

—Terri Guillemets

*Let us therefore make every effort to do what leads to peace and mutual edification.*

—Romans 14:19

# Build Relationships

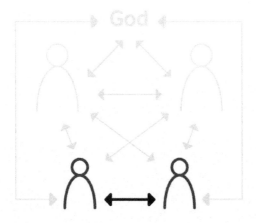

# 8

---

## SIBLINGS AS BEST FRIENDS

A young lady from our church was at our home recently. While she was there, some of our girls were home from college for the weekend—so she was there with about five of the Manning kids. Her mom came up to Suzanne a few days later and said, "My daughter came home from your house and she said, 'Those Mannings sure do like being around each other!'"

How did this happen in our family? Although we're not without conflict in our home, we can say without a doubt our kids love each other and have a lot of fun together. Having kids who get along is such a cool thing to have in a family!

I have to admit, I had no clue when I started my family that kids could get along so well. It certainly was not my experience growing up. I just assumed that all siblings fought as kids and then maybe the relationship got better when they were adults.

But then we saw some families who were different, and we heard someone teach us what we'll now tell you in a CCC:

SIBLINGS CAN AND SHOULD BE BEST FRIENDS FOR LIFE!

# To Love *and* Like Each Other

Just as teenage rebellion should be the exception rather than the rule, in a Crazy Cool Family, siblings should be trained and developed to not only love each other but to like each other as well. Siblings can and should be the best of friends throughout their lives.

I know what you may be thinking. What? Are you serious? What have these guys been smoking? Don't they know about sibling rivalry? Don't they know *all* siblings fight like crazy until they're adults, and maybe *then* they'll start to love and respect each other? I know those thoughts, the disbelief—because I was there! It was a tough sell for me, too, believing I could teach my kids to become the best of friends... for life.

But here's a powerful truth I discovered: What we write on the hearts of our children tends to stay there. They're like a large dry erase board, and we have the opportunity to write whatever we choose onto their hearts. We need to be careful—some of what we write there can be to their detriment, bruising, or wounding of their hearts. But if we're intentional, choosing to write the good stuff, they'll carry those blessings forward in life.

Proverbs 1:8-9 offers this wisdom: *"Listen, my son, to your father's instruction and do not forsake your mother's teaching. They are a garland to grace your head and a chain to adorn your neck."* So, Mom, Dad—what instruction, what attitudes are you conveying to your children?

From their earliest days, we should instill in our children the understanding that God put brothers and sisters into the family for a reason, just like He put Mom and Dad there. Not only is it very possible for siblings to love each other throughout their lives, it's God's intent and design.

## Hard-Wired for Family

You'd think people who've been wounded by family would look to run far away into the arms of others, totally and completely rejecting everything having to do with their family. Yet, so often, those who have been abused and hurt by key family members still cherish the idea of family and desire to keep the idea of family alive. I believe the reason this happens is we're hard-wired by the Lord for family.

The first mention of family is in Genesis 2, when the two become one flesh. When the flood came, God didn't just save Noah (Genesis 6:18) but his entire family. When God called Abraham out of Haran, He called him and his family (Genesis 12:4-5). From two of the Ten Commandments—honoring father and mother and prohibiting adultery—flow many of the Mosaic laws that seek to protect marriage and the family. Jesus speaks against divorce. Paul affirms and expands on the two commandments. All throughout our Bible, God affirms family.

God has planted within us a fierce longing for a family that is safe and healthy. It's this desire that makes children continue to want the approval of a parent even after they've been abandoned or abused by that parent. We all long to belong to a family. We all want our independence at some point, but what we really want is to

*God has planted within us a fierce longing for a family that is safe and healthy.*

launch into our independence from a healthy base point. In addition to the independence, we want the security of belonging. We all want a family which provides a secure safety net we can fall back on in times of trouble—a safe place to celebrate our successes and heal from our failures.

We believe God wants us, as parents, to take this hard-wired love of family in our children's hearts and nurture it with purpose. The unity, safety, and closeness of our family has been a priority in our parenting for many years. We've seen great success. In fact, when we asked Michael, our then 14-year-old son, who his best friends were, he replied, "My sisters, I guess." Does that seem like a weird answer? If you knew Michael, you'd realize he's one of the most popular, well-liked, well-adjusted teenagers you could meet. He's a leader and a strong personality in his grade. He has many great friends. But he also really loves his sisters, and he hangs out with them at home, at school, wherever. His sisters have invested in him, too. They genuinely like him and like being around him. When Suzanne asked him who his best friends were, he wasn't trying to impress his mom. His sisters were just his first thought, the legit answer to the question.

When we train our children in the importance of family bonding and family unity, it takes that hard-wired family desire God put within us and allows it to flourish as God intended. Over time, that healthy desire takes on a life of its own as your children start to believe in it and pursue each other. When we purpose as parents to nurture that desire, making it a priority in our family, we kindle a small fire which will start to burn brighter and brighter in our homes.

When our oldest daughter Mollie was twelve or thirteen and our next daughter Madeline was about eight or nine, they didn't get along. Their personalities are totally different. Mollie is very organized and particular, while Madeline is much more of a free spirit. Both were obedient, godly kids, but they just had very different personalities. You can imagine the setting: Mollie was in the beginning stages of her teenage years and Madeline was an annoying younger sibling, trying so hard to be accepted and liked by others. She especially wanted the attention of her older sister, whom she both idolized...and irritated. Not exactly the best setting in which to cultivate siblings becoming best friends.

Suzanne and I kept encouraging our daughters to pursue each other. We told Mollie how important she was to Madeline's development. We had the talk so many times—it always went something like this: "Mollie, I know it's tough to like your sister sometimes..."—at this point her facial expression would all but shout, 'You mean ALL THE TIME!'—"I know your age difference and personality differences make this relationship a challenge. But Mollie, I need you to understand how important you are for Madeline to be healthy emotionally and spiritually. She so looks up to you. You have a very special place in her heart. In fact, other than Mom and me, there's no one who will have more impact in her life right now than you. When you reject her or are mean to her, it damages her heart, and puts a wound there that tells her she is not good enough and that she doesn't have what it takes. But when you love her and include her, even when you don't want to and don't feel like it, you're telling her how special she is. You're telling her she belongs, and that she's worth having around. There's no one more important than you for Madeline to hear that from. The way to help her not be annoying is not to reject her, but to include her. Over time as you include her, she won't fight for your attention so much, and you'll come to appreciate her more."

*When we consistently encourage and gently require our children to turn towards each other, over time they respond.*

Are you bored with my fatherly talk yet? I'm sure Mollie was too but think of the alternative. So often when siblings fight, parents respond with frustration and control: "Stop fighting with your brother! I can't stand it! Now you let him play with you and your friend! No arguing! You go play right now... and include your brother like I asked!" Sound familiar? I know I've been there, said it, done it. The trouble is, we've just made the situation worse, creating even more tension and resentment. Not only does the older child not understand why he must play with the younger sibling, but he's also now filled with resentment towards his brother. We've just set up the younger sibling for even more abuse. We've made things worse. Sad but true.

When we consistently encourage and gently require our children to turn towards each other, over time they respond.

Children are smart. When they understand the outcome of their actions, and we sink the vision deep in their hearts, they'll see it. They love their siblings and don't want to see them hurt. If we show them a pathway to success and show them the incredible importance of the role they play in their siblings' lives, they think about more than themselves.

We would also focus on the younger sibling as well. The talk Madeline received centered around coaching her how not to be annoying and how to respect her older sister, especially when Mollie was with her friends. We encouraged Madeline if she wanted to be included, she needed to make sure she honored Mollie and wasn't being obnoxious, silly, or demanding her own way. She needed to be fun and full of life and try to go with the flow as she learned to play like the big girls.

The outcome? These two sisters are now truly great friends.

**MOLLIE: I can understand how nuts it is to think your kids can be best friends. I thought that for a large part of my life, too. The age gap between Madeline and me is four and half years and, to me, grew larger as we got older. It started when she became annoying to have her around my friends and didn't stop until well into my high school years. I was adamant, but so were Mom and Dad. "Your sister will be your best friend." They were diligent in encouraging us to pursue each other. They always reminded us Jesus gave us each other to be best friends. I thought it was absurd. My best friends and I went shopping, we spent the night together, we talked about boys. No way would I do those things with Madeline. My junior year of high school, for whatever reason, probably God's sovereign plan, I had to take Madeline to school. That 20-minute ride forced togetherness. We talked about school, tests, and boys. We started to like the same music and ask each other advice. Mom and Dad were right. In that year, Madeline became my best friend. That summer, we chose to spend time together—Sonic runs, babysitting, shopping. All the things I found in my *best friends*, I now found in Madeline.**

I was too caught up in my own world, in the lie that our age difference was too big a span, that our paths didn't cross, and that they never would. I couldn't see past what was happening in my life at that time to know future Mollie would need Madeline as her sister, and more importantly, her best friend. But my parents saw it. They were in tune to the importance of siblings being best friends, and they tirelessly fought for it. I can only imagine they wanted to give up as much as I wanted to not be Madeline's friend. Our endless fights, my frequent sass, Madeline's tears—it wasn't easy to encourage us to pursue one another, and I know the battle wasn't won in front of Madeline and me. My parents took it to the Lord. They battled for us in the spiritual realm when we were too young, too selfish, and too blind to do it on our own.

While the car rides to school were pivotal for Madeline and me, something else was happening. We were forming our own individual relationships with Jesus, which truly set the foundation for us to build a best friendship. As we grew up and developed our personal relationships with God, we began to experience spiritual growth together—a bonus that didn't occur to me in the talks of boys, clothes, and music. Madeline, like all my siblings, challenges my faith. Our being best friends doesn't stop at group messages, FaceTime, and memories. It goes beyond that into what Jesus is doing in our lives and what He's saying to each one of us, sometimes even about the other. That, I have to believe, is why my parents kept the fight alive when the relationship seemed beyond repair. They knew that believing in Jesus is a connector, a common ground maker, and they knew in time we'd discover that.

I have a unique perspective into this idea, too, because I have two little brothers from my dad and stepmom (the King family). So, when I say *all* my siblings are my best friends, I mean all eight of them. You might be thinking, "Well, this worked with your siblings, but how do you know it will work for other families, other situations, or people who live life differently?" I know it will because I've lived it. Jordan and Joshua (my stepbrothers) are the same ages as McKenzie and Michael, and there's a large age gap there, too. But in this situation, there are so many other things the world might say that would create a divide in my relationships with them. We didn't live in the same house growing up, our parents disciplined us differently, I saw them less, etc. But as I began to buy into this idea of siblings as my best friends, it transferred to all my sibling relationships.

I think my parents knew, "win one over and we'll get 'em all!" Once Madeline and I became best friends, it was just what we did. Mannings were best friends with each other; it became part of our family culture.

When I went to college, I joined a sorority. Everyone kept saying these girls would be my sisters. I sat there thinking, "I already have three amazing sisters; I don't need anymore!" Of course, I drank the Kool-Aid, and I'm still close with a few sorority sisters today. But as Dad says, "Friends come and go, but siblings are for forever." My sisters and I now live three hours apart. We run the spectrum of life phases, but we talk all the time. We text funny things to each other, we ask for prayer requests, we tell each other things that happened during the day... you know, things you do with your best friends.

It's important to lay the groundwork for your kids as soon as you can. When we were little, I was old enough to comprehend Macy and Madeline were my sisters, and I knew they affected my life, but I was too young to understand the spiritual effect they would have on me. But Mom and Dad knew this all along and did not allow worldly excuses to get in the way. Parents, age is not an excuse. Different seasons of life is not an excuse. Fighting, boys and girls, halfsiblings, not excuses. Like Dad said, "God designed your family, beautifully and perfectly, before even the beginning of time, and part of that design is for your children to be best friends with one another."

My parents made this idea simple. They used to say, "You'll be best friends with your siblings. Jesus gave them to you. He called you to love them, and they'll be one of the biggest sources of joy in your life." We can all probably say that in our sleep because of how often we heard it!

With sisters, it's easy to bond over things you have in common, right? Girl stuff. With boys, it might be a little harder—again, a worldly excuse my parents never entertained. Since I'm the oldest and the boys came last, our age range is comical. Cade is 17 years younger than me, with Michael and Maddox in between. I used to make them call me "Miss Mollie" when I took them out because "Mollie" and "Mommy" sound the same coming from a baby's mouth. I used to get lots of funny stares. Cade will often ask something along the lines of, "Mollie, will you be 50 when I graduate?" Not quite kid! I'm sure at times they felt like I was more of a mom than a friend, but in our house now, when we are all together, they're as much our best friends as we are theirs.

Your daughter can be best friends with her brother, and your son can learn to cherish and protect his sister. Don't allow the excuses of worldly relationships into the design God has created for your family. The groundwork has been given to you. Go and take it.

I know it sounds like we might never fight, or we have no issues or wounds—which is not the case. When you have a family of nine people, or with any group of any amount, there will be differences. Differences in the very least of which are personalities and boys versus girls. In our case, differences have surfaced when we talk about churches, relationships, how we spend money, and what is worldly and what is not. There are wounds that have come from these kinds of disagreements and conversations, which we've had to discuss and heal from. Relationships are a never-ending process of learning and growing.

Relationships that are worth fighting for won't happen overnight. It took Madeline and me 16 years. They also won't happen accidently. I know my parents had this as a vision for their family from the beginning. This might be the first time you're hearing this idea, or maybe it's a vision you've had for your family, too. Wherever you're at, as long as you understand it's importance, the power of prayer, persistence, and living the relationships you desire for your kids, you'll see the fruit in your family's lives. It's not an easy feat, but the reward is so worth it.

From our oldest to our youngest...

McCADE: Maddox is my best friend because he always plays with me when I want him to play. He helps me with everything. He helps me study my spelling and other school stuff. He practices with me at whatever sport we're playing. He shares everything he has with me. He lets me sleep in his room whenever I want. Mostly he looks out for me.

Michael takes me to Sonic and spends his own money on me. I think that's a big deal because he has worked hard for the money and he's used that money on me. His nickname for me is "kid."

Dinners with all the sisters can be so boring! All they talk about is adult stuff like money and marriage and house stuff. But just when I am about to leave the table, they ask me questions about me because they like me.

MACY: I remember growing up with McKenzie by my side, and I was not upset about it. There was never a moment we were separated, and we didn't understand the concept of "my own friends." When her friends came over, I had freedom to play with them or not. We had several families whose children were near the same age as Kenzie and me. We were always both invited to their houses or birthday parties. We went everywhere together; some would say we were a package deal. This fostered a friendship between Kenzie and me. I remember one weekend when McKenzie and I went to a birthday party at a friend's house. As the night unfolded, we started to feel uncomfortable with the party theme and the movie they chose to watch. We had each other and felt comfortable to call our mom to come get us. I knew I had McKenzie, and she would stick by me no matter what. Mom always said, "It's easier to stand alone when you are standing with someone."

I've also seen this play out with my littlest brothers, Maddox and McCade. Even though Maddox is a few years older, he was invited to all of McCade's friends' birthday parties, and he went because he was friends with all of those little boys. Keeping the siblings together encourages a strong friendship between them, as well as all their friends. A practical way for parents to promote "best friendship" between siblings is to create opportunities for them to hang out together. Now, this may seem hard to do if they don't like each other, but when you start them young and being together becomes their norm, they'll get used to being together. I really believe the amount of time I spent with my sisters created the friendships I have with them today. I did everything with them growing up, and all of my memories include them. No matter what happens today, I'll always have those memories to help me love them through every season. I'm convinced they'll always be there for me, and that foundation was built from my childhood and all the time we spent together learning to be friends, no matter what.

## Different is Good

I don't think I've ever heard a mom or dad say, "We have three kids, and they're all so similar. I can't believe how much they're alike!" Instead, you always hear how different they are. Every parent shares how amazed they are that such different children came from the same parents. Ever wonder why God made our kids so different?

In case you were wondering, the uniqueness and differences don't start to even out when you get to seven kids. Suzanne and I would say the same thing—our kids are all so different. And I'm convinced God demonstrates His great sense of humor in these things.

**SUZANNE: We have three introverts and four extroverts (or as McCade calls them, outroverts). All range in athletic ability. A couple of our kids have learning differences, one is musically talented, another can draw and paint beautifully—all the illustrations in this book are drawn by her. A couple are amazing at puzzles. A few are detail-oriented and others are anti-detail. The list of differences goes on and on. It's what makes family so dynamic, interesting, and fun. One of my many favorite things about newborns is the wonder of what they'll be like when they grow up and how they'll fit into and bless their family and the world.**

Like you—like all parents—we deal with a diversity of personalities and character traits in our home. To add to it, Suzanne and I are also very different people. She has a much more sensitive spirit and is more people-oriented. I'm more analytical, and while I love people, I'm definitely less emotional with them. She loves to stay at home, and I like to go places. She lives in the moment, and I'm always looking ahead. Even after many years of marriage, communication can be difficult sometimes. We like different things, and we definitely think differently. I suppose it's that way in most marriages. Suzanne and I weren't attracted to someone like ourselves. We were attracted to and married someone who was markedly different in personality and temperament. We love each other. We're committed to each other. And our marriage has grown over the years through our differences.

If you believe the apostle Paul's argument in Acts 17:26, *"From one man he made all the nations, that they should inhabit the whole earth; and he marked out their appointed times in history and the boundaries of their lands,"* the natural implication is that God orchestrated your place, too, within your family. Diversity and all. It's no accident or coincidence.

So, what do you do with all the diversity in your home? We believe God put it there for a reason, so we need to celebrate and learn from it. If God made attraction to different personalities the norm in marriage and then consistently gives families children with great diversity, then He must have a reason for it. He could very easily have made us all cookie-cutter-clones within the family. He could have made men and women the same. We could be attracted to a similar mate, and then we could have all our kids be the same. But it's obvious He didn't make our world that way. In fact, as the evidence all around us overwhelmingly testifies, our God is a God who creates and celebrates uniqueness! We should do the same.

God doesn't give us clones in our families to make it easy. Instead, He gives us a very diverse mixture of  people, personalities, and passions so we can have a laboratory in which to learn... so that we have great spiritual success out in the world. Our families are training grounds for us to learn to play well with others.

*Families are training grounds for us to learn to play well with others.*

Our families are like a Petri dish. Scientists use Petri dishes to grow things in a controlled environment before testing them in the harsher conditions of the outside world. In the same way, our families are controlled environments where our children can be built up and learn to handle life's situations well. It's a fertile training ground with endless opportunities for nurturing and growth.

We frequently tell our children they must learn to get along with their siblings so they can get along with the outside world. If they can master it at home with their very different siblings, people older and younger and with very diverse interests, then they will be well-equipped to handle everyone they encounter as they grow up.

SUZANNE: One of the things I always tell my children is, "figure out a way to get along." God has put specific sibling relationships into their lives to train, teach, and draw them to be like Jesus. If they can master a personality type that totally gets on their nerves, they're a better person for it. If they continue to create conflict, I have found God is faithful to put that personality type into their lives again and again—a friend, coach, teacher, employer, roommate, and if need be, a spouse, child or grandchild. This really motivates them to choose ways to successfully and peacefully connect with even the most trying or annoying of personality types.

I believe God puts people in our lives to give us opportunities to learn how to love at all different levels. When we have a hard time extending love and acceptance to that impossible person, then it's a great chance to cry out to God for His help showing love to the unlovable.

"Let us love one another, for love comes from God" (1 John 4:7). We also emphasize how important it is for our children to take care of the hearts of their siblings. The world is going to do enough damage to their siblings. Do they want to be a brother or sister who adds to that heartache, or do they want to be a healer for their siblings? By treating their siblings with love and respect and looking out for them instead of arguing and fighting with them, they speak health and life into their hearts, not damage and death. The greater good of their siblings starts to resonate in their hearts, and they start to defend and help each other rather than hurt each other. Does it totally eliminate sibling conflict? Absolutely not.

But we can say without a doubt that teaching sibling unity definitely minimizes sibling conflict, gives us a strong tool to counteract it, and encourages siblings to invest in each other over tearing each other down. Here it is, encapsulated in a CCC:

> GOD USES SIBLING RELATIONSHIPS TO TRAIN OUR
> CHILDREN FOR REAL WORLD RELATIONSHIPS.

# Influence

As human beings, we tend to focus on the shortcomings of others. We focus on trying to avoid the irritations that frequently manifest themselves whenever we're around that person. In families, those shortcomings are magnified. If they talk too much or are selfish or their room is not clean or whatever the fault is, when we are annoyed with a family member, those shortcomings can be really annoying.

To counteract this tendency within our family, we turn the tables with our children and have them focus on giving their gifts to their siblings instead of focusing on the shortcomings. It's amazing what can happen when we focus on turning their hearts away from themselves and onto their siblings. Instead of focusing on others' faults which are so easy to find, we encourage them to focus instead on what they are going to give to their siblings in order to love them and help them grow spiritually.

For example, when Michael, our oldest son, was 13 years old and Maddox was nine, they were having trouble getting along. Like Mollie and Madeline before them, they have very different personalities. Michael is more secure and leadership-oriented, while Maddox is more analytical and hard-working. It's interesting for us as parents to recall; it was at this same age that Mollie and Madeline were having their greatest conflicts.

I was playing basketball with them. Michael is a good athlete that exudes confidence. Maddox is also a good athlete, but he is the type that is harder on himself. As we played, I noticed Michael making some critical comments to Maddox, and Maddox wasn't taking it well. Michael also used his height and strength advantage a little too much. Maddox was frustrated… and agitated.

I pulled Michael aside and told him one of his greatest assets was his confidence. As his dad, I loved his belief in himself and the way he carried himself on the court and in life. When I called him over, you could tell he was expecting a lecture. When I praised him instead, he became receptive to my comments. What he didn't know was I was setting the hook. Hook set—it was time to reel it in.

"Wouldn't it be great, Michael," I asked, "if you could give some of your confidence to Maddox? What if, because of your influence, Maddox became the most confident basketball player in his grade? No dad would be happier than me if I could tell others how his confidence soared because of his big brother's influence. Wouldn't that be cool? What do you need to do to make that happen? Do you think you should look for the good in him and encourage him? Or do you think you should criticize him?"

I offered to Michael, "I'll be the coach/dad and handle the criticism. How about you focus on being the most encouraging big brother you can be and see if you can transfer your incredible confidence to him? That would be an awesome gift you could give him!"

Did it work? Sort of. Raising children is not an arena of instant gratification. We try to instill tracks in their brains and hearts which, over time, become ingrained into their way of thinking. It happens inch-by-inch over time.

*Your kids can and should be great friends at every stage of life.*

Your kids can and should be great friends at every stage of life. It can work with siblings close in age, all the way to kids like Mollie and McCade with 17 years between them. As parents, our job is to believe it can happen, expect it in our families, and encourage it consistently. God created our diverse families as an incredible laboratory for creating life-giving kids who love and like each other. This united family is a lot of fun, and creates a strong, lifelong base to launch our children into the world.

# Create Culture

| Encourage | Safe | Disciple | Unity |
|-----------|------|----------|-------|

# SECTION THREE: CREATE CULTURE

We keep digging a little deeper. First, we talked about your relationship with God. About how the best parents are beloved sons and daughters first.

Then we talked a lot about all of the relationships in our home. That the quality of our family will be determined by the quality of the relationships.

Now it gets even more fun. Crazy Cool Families create a culture where relationships can flourish. What is culture? Webster says it is "the integrated pattern of human knowledge, belief, and behavior that depends upon the capacity for learning and transmitting knowledge to succeeding generations."

That's a little wordy for me. I like the "succeeding generations" part, though. The rest is true but a little above my head. Culture is how your home *feels*. It's the atmosphere.

Let me ask you some questions. Is your home life-giving or death-giving? Engaging or harsh? Free or oppressive? Characterized by laughing or fighting? Filled with grace or condemnation?

Last question about your home: Do you want to be there, or do you want to escape?

Home is the last place many of us want to go, but home can be your favorite place in the world! As parents, we get the incredible opportunity to create this culture any way we want! And we have a God who loves nothing better than to show us how to create that culture in His image!

Culture is more practical. It's the how to the why. It's the details to the big picture. Come dig a little deeper with us. We really are going to show you how to make home your favorite place in the world!

# en·cour·age·ment

/inˈkərijmənt/ /enˈkərijmənt/

noun

the action of giving someone support, confidence, or hope

*"When you encourage others, you in the process are encouraged because you're making a commitment and difference in that person's life. Encouragement really does make a difference."*
—Zig Ziglar

*"Our chief want is someone who will inspire us to be what we know we could be."*
—Ralph Waldo Emerson

*But encourage one another daily, as long as it is called "Today," so that none of you may be hardened by sin's deceitfulness.*
—Hebrews 3:13

# Create Culture

| **Encourage** | Safe | Disciple | Unity |

# 9

## ENCOURAGE EXTRAVAGANTLY AND CORRECT CAREFULLY

In 1940, an African American girl was born prematurely to a family in Tennessee. She was the 20th of 22 children. Her father was a railroad porter, and her mother cleaned houses. The girl contracted a form of polio at a young age which led to a condition known as Infantile Paralysis. Doctors told her parents she would never walk again.

Her mother told her little girl differently. She encouraged her daughter she would absolutely walk again and took her on 50-mile bus rides twice a week for several years to go to therapy. She had 19 other children when this child was born, added a couple more after her, and worked tirelessly to provide for her family. If anyone was entitled to a give up, I think it would be this mom.

Instead she rallied the family around her stricken daughter. Doctors told her to massage her daughter's legs four times a day. She enlisted all her children to help. They bought her braces to help her walk. By the time she was eight years old, the girl could walk with the aid of the braces. Her mother kept encouraging her, "Never give up!"

Imagine the mother's delight when one day she came home and found her daughter walking without the braces. At that point, in a real-life Forrest Gump story, her now 11-year-old daughter started running and never stopped. She ran so well that by the time she was 16, she qualified for the 1956 Olympics.

The girl's name: Wilma Rudolph. In the 1960 Olympics, she won gold medals in the 100M, 200M, and 400M relay. The girl who would never walk again was now the fastest woman in the world.

When reporters asked how she overcame her disability, she said, "My doctor told me I would never walk again. My momma told me I would. I believed my momma."

Wilma Rudolph's amazing mother knew the power of encouragement. She believed in her daughter, and her God, in spite of the circumstances. Because of her mother's belief in her, Wilma was able to overcome her obstacles and became one of the finest athletes of her generation. Her mom had every excuse to be discouraging, but she chose differently.

## The Power of Encouragement

In creating the culture in your home, never underestimate the power of encouragement and the danger of excessive correction. Let me give you a CCC that echoes this chapter's title:

> WE ENCOURAGE EXTRAVAGANTLY AND CORRECT CAREFULLY TO OPEN UP THE HEARTS OF OUR CHILDREN.

When we do conferences, many times we start by encouraging them. It's so practical, and it's a tool you can employ immediately. A heart change in this area will have an immediate positive impact in our home.

The Bible says, "Encourage one another daily, as long as it is called Today, so that none of you may be hardened by sin's deceitfulness" (Hebrews 3:13). Parse that out: we are to "encourage one another daily," or in other words, frequently.

For "as long as it is called Today," or in other words, as long as we are on this earth. Why? "So that" our hearts will not be hardened by sin.

Encouragement is so important to God that He includes it as a spiritual gift. The apostle Paul said so: *"We have different gifts, according to the grace given to each of us. If your gift is prophesying, then prophesy in accordance with your faith; if it is serving, then serve; if it is teaching, then teach, IF IT IS TO ENCOURAGE, THEN GIVE ENCOURAGEMENT; if it is giving, then give generously; if it is to lead, do it diligently; if it is to show mercy, do it cheerfully"* (Romans 12:6-8, emphasis mine).

Encouragement is given as a gift from the Lord and with good reason. Encouragement opens up the heart!

**SUZANNE: To encourage means to fill someone up with courage; to put courage "into" them. That is so powerful to practice! We need a crazy amount of courage to succeed in this discouraging world we live in!**

*I was changing from a fearful, critical dad, to a faith-filled, believing dad.*

Notice Suzanne used the word "discouraging." Where encouraging is to put courage into someone, discouraging is to take courage out of someone.

In my early years as a parent, I was all about obedience and character, whether it was school or sports or life. I made sure my children knew about their mistakes so they could correct them. It makes sense, right? How are they going to know how to correct their errors if I, as the parent, don't point them out? The more I correct them, the better it is for them.

What I didn't recognize at first was how our kids would subtly—or sometimes not so subtly—go with Mom after their ball game to avoid the "helpful advice" from Dad. They loved me but resented and maybe even feared my corrective presence.

As I realized the negative impact of my zeal for perfection, I determined to lecture less. I looked to encourage and build relationships with my children instead of always examining and correcting their performance. A few years ago, I really saw the positive impact of my encouragement efforts. I was driving in the car with my then 16-year-old daughter, Madeline. We were talking, and she said something I will never forget: "Dad, five years ago I didn't think I could do anything right in your eyes. Now I don't think I could do anything wrong!"

What could make my daughter say that? I'll tell you—before, she felt as if I was always looking to point out what she'd done wrong. As my focus changed, she began to see her father as one who believed in her. It was absolutely true; I saw my daughter differently. And I wasn't just looking at her differently. I was looking at life differently. I was changing from a fearful, critical dad, to a faith-filled, believing dad.

**MOLLIE: There are lots of personalities in our household, lots of strong ones at that. Macy and I are the "emotional ones." When Dad would get onto us for not doing the dishes, being mean to a sibling, or talking back to Mom, we'd burst into tears. Almost on cue—but these were legitimate tears. We felt our feelings were hurt, and Dad had wronged us in some way. Dad could never get through to his parenting point because it would get washed away in the mix of hysterics and tears.**

**This went on for quite some time. Back and forth we'd go, lectures led to tears which led to Dad somewhat apologizing, and Macy and I somewhat accepting. All parties walked away unsatisfied with the result. But lucky for us, Dad realized he needed to change, and God was the only person who was going to be able to do that. Dad realized in order to see his family flourish and in order to be what God had called him to be—a parent to two very emotional females—he had to rely fully on who God had called him to be, not what *he thought* parenting should be. You might be thinking that as our parent, Dad was in his parameters to correct us, to discipline, lecture, and get on**

to us. You might also think this many times in the middle of a pity party or tantrum with your child; you have the right, and so did Dad. But that wasn't Dad's focus. He left behind the idea that *he* could decide how to parent, *his* ideas on how *he* saw us, and what *he* thought we needed. Instead, he started to partner with God on what it looked like to raise the daughters God had given him. In this back and forth, God released the spirit of criticism from Dad and replaced it with one of encouragement. He opened Dad's eyes to see us the way that He did.

And we saw the transformation. Getting in trouble after this became much more about how Dad loved us and wanted us to succeed than what we had done wrong. Mace and I are both still avid criers, but we're also avid supporters of our dad and how he allowed himself to be molded into a better follower of Jesus, into a better man, which then molded him into a better dad.

I'm grateful for the compliments of my daughter, but let me tell you, the changes in me didn't come easy. Suzanne would tell me I was getting on them too harshly, and I'd respond with something like, "Well if I don't get on to them, how are they going to know what they did wrong? And maybe if you would get on them instead of me, then I wouldn't have to get on them so much!" Worked great for my marriage, as you might imagine.

I wasn't only frustrated with my wife for calling me out, but I had four daughters! It seemed like I couldn't even feel angry without everyone running for the exits; like there was an anger sensor in my home, or an alarm sounded whenever I got the least bit upset. It was annoying. Frustrating. Suffocating, even. As I processed it with the Lord, I realized He cared so much about my critical spirit and the damage it was doing to my family that He put five women in my life so I could practice being sensitive to them. I had to change my heart-view of how correction worked. My criticism was ineffective because of its repetition and tone. Reducing my criticism and becoming more encouraging got my kids to listen more and actually hear what

I was trying to get through to them.

In the book, *Sacred Parenting*, Gary Thomas says, "We live in the midst of holy teachers. Sometimes they spit up on themselves or on us. Sometimes they throw tantrums. Sometimes they cuddle us and kiss us and love us. In the good and the bad, they mold our hearts, shape our souls, and invite us to experience God in newer and deeper ways."

God uses our kids to change us, so we can turn around and encourage them.

**SUZANNE: We must be our child's biggest cheerleader! They need to know that they have no bigger fan in the world than me as their mother. I love them, I believe in them, and I absolutely desire the best for their lives.**

**We cannot depend on the world to build them up! In fact, the world seems bent on tearing them down most of the time. From ads on TV telling them they're not pretty, smart, or thin enough, to petty drama among peers**

*The best thing I can do for them is to restore them to their greatness and remind them of how wonderful they are and how much I love them.*

**and even friends, our children are usually not being built up outside of our home. When they come into my house, they're coming from a world that's mean, sometimes scary, and many times difficult and emotionally draining. They don't need me to add to this harshness. The world gives them enough of that. The best thing I can do for them is to restore them to their greatness and remind them of how wonderful they are and how much I love them.**

**Isn't that what God does for us? He doesn't focus on our faults, our failings, or our inadequacies. He doesn't lecture us on how to get better, do more, shape up, get on the team. He doesn't bring us in for a "pep talk." His advice to**

us is to remind us of who we are—we are His children, empowered by His Holy Spirit, and wrapped in His love. We have been saved by His grace through His Son.

The best thing we can do is to follow God's example. We remind our children who they are in Christ and who they are in our family. Our job as parents is not to add to or compound the pain the world causes. Instead, just as God is life-giving to us, we should flow with life to our children. One of my most important roles as a mother is to be an encourager to my child. I need to focus and bring out their strengths and not focus on their weaknesses. I need to love them unconditionally and let them know they're special in God's eyes and mine.

McKENZIE: Being there for your children is an essential part of an encouraging culture. A concept I learned in a class is called pronoia. It is when you are completely for someone—when you use uplifting, positive words and actions.

Pronoia doesn't just happen, you have to fight for it! Are you for your children? Your words, in front of them and behind closed doors, affect the way they see themselves. You have to be their biggest fan. When I know my parents, family, and friends are totally for me, then it seems like the whole world is for me.

We must understand words aren't neutral. God spent a lot of time in the Bible telling their people who they are, not who they're not! God called Abraham a father of many nations. He called Gideon a mighty warrior. Jesus called Peter a Rock and restored him, even after he denied Jesus three times. Here's a CCC:

> GOD, OUR FATHER, SEES US AS WHO WE
> ARE AND SPEAKS IT INTO US. WE SHOULD
> DO THE SAME FOR OUR CHILDREN.

Listen to Macy's perspective on being encouraged as a little girl in the Manning family.

MACY: There was a season of my life when I hated clothes. I hated getting dressed, picking outfits, and looking in the mirror. I was going through a growth spurt, or as me and my family say now, my "fat stage." We all laugh about it now, and I can handle it because I have a confidence that is not of this world. My confidence comes from Jesus Christ, and I see myself the way He sees me. When I was growing up, my family, especially the girls, helped me believe that.

I remember countless Sunday mornings I'd walk into my mom's bathroom in hysterical tears because I felt fat. Mollie usually picked my outfit out, and she'd patiently pick out as many outfits as I needed until I felt comfortable. I think my family encouraged me not to believe the lies the enemy was telling me. I had countless thoughts throughout the day about my weight, but I never received any negativity from my family. No one called me ugly, fat, or overweight. They encouraged me and never treated me differently. I was their sister and their friend.

I love encouragement. I believe the easiest way to give encouragement is with words, but there are other ways. My sisters were patient with me when I had meltdowns. They gave me advice on accessories and shoes. They loved me even when I didn't love myself, and that was encouraging. Eventually, I thinned out, and as my faith grew, so did my confidence in my physical appearance. My season of life did not define me, and my family helped me by doing life alongside me and supporting me. Their encouragement was not always verbal, but through their actions and demeanor, I always felt accepted and loved.

Macy said something there that I want to make sure doesn't go unnoticed. She said, "My season of life did not define me." So often our children go through stages of life they will grow out of eventually. Maybe it's a physical issue, maybe it's an emotional fear, or maybe it's a spiritual question. If we're critical and discouraging in these times, we make these stages into wounds that have long-term impacts on their hearts. When we encourage them through these stages, we can turn these negative seasons into areas of their lives they remember for being an overcomer rather than a failure.

I remember Suzanne coming to me overwhelmed by Macy's meltdowns. It's so hard as a parent to see your child suffer. But Suzanne knew she had to be encouraging in those moments with Macy, to help Macy see herself differently. Suzanne used that time to teach each of our daughters how to be encouraging as well. These difficult stages of life are inevitable. We're at our best as parents when we turn these stages into opportunities for encouragement and opportunities to teach our kids valuable life lessons.

And from the boys, here are perspectives from Maddox and McCade.

> **MADDOX: My parents encourage me every day. When I played baseball, my dad was the head coach. All the other dads would yell at their kids, but my dad didn't ever yell at me. He encouraged me first, then he would add his advice on how I played. One time I came back from a basketball tournament, and I played badly. But in the car on our way home, he said I ran the offense right and played good defense. Then he said my elbow was out on my shot, the perfect mixture of encouragement and critique.**

> **McCADE: Encouragement means to bring people up. My parents really encourage me by saying nice job or good job when I do something well. Another way they encourage me is when they cheer really loud at my football and basketball games. Encouragement feels like I just got something, like a present I really wanted.**

By the way, while both of those statements are true from the boys, they're not entirely accurate. My boys are being generous towards their dad. When I coach their teams, I am pretty intense, and I definitely get onto them. But what I can say is I'm generally a much more encouraging coach today than I was when the girls were young. And I appreciate this is the perception of my boys. Because I've moved in the direction of encouragement, they see me as very encouraging. Even "perfect" in the words of Maddox. As we start to encourage and speak life into our kids—"bring them up," in the words of McCade—the encouragement we give them not only helps their heart, but it also makes them see us as their heroes instead of their chief critics!

> **SUZANNE: We started this section saying we usually open our conferences with encouragement. I'd like to end this section by encouraging you:**
> **You are an amazing parent... the perfect person to raise the children you've been entrusted with. God has given you every good gift that you need to train up your child to be who God has created them to be. Before time began, God knew you would be the best parent for your child. You would be the one to point them to Him in a mighty way. You're the one He picked to do the fun, hard, easy, and painful details of life with the little people that He hand-picked just for you. He has a beautiful journey of faith and love designed for your family. He chose you and your children for greatness. Believe.**

## Curb the Correction

Being an encouraging parent is a game changer. Becoming an encouraging parent means we encourage more, correct less, and really watch the way we correct. So how do you stop being critical? Simple—just stop. I'm not kidding. When you feel the urge to be critical, just bite your tongue. It will be tough at first and seem like you're missing so many great opportunities to instruct your child, or spouse for that matter. But just be quiet. Almost every parent I know corrects too much, too harshly, and at the wrong times. Just stop until you can get it under control. Then after a while—probably a long while—you can start to reintroduce it in a healthier way as God reveals more to you.

Remember how we said earlier the best parents are beloved sons and daughters? This is a great example of living out your relationship with God. God tells us to be encouraging, and we work to change our thoughts and actions to align ourselves with His ways of thinking. Suzanne shares it this way:

> **SUZANNE: Scripture says to take every thought captive.** *"We destroy every proud obstacle that keeps people from knowing God. We capture their rebellious thoughts and teach them to obey Christ"* **(2 Corinthians 10:5 NLT).**
>
> Critical thoughts are great thoughts to take captive. Believe me, it's hard to pay attention to your thoughts let alone change them, but it's possible. The first step is to pay attention to your thoughts so when a critical thought comes in, you recognize it. Next comes the fun part: flip it! Turn the critical thought into a positive thought, and then say *that* thought out loud.
>
> I'll give you an example: "My child is such a slob. He gets food all over his mouth every time he eats. People probably think he's a pig." Critical thought—agreed? Take that thought captive. Use self-control, and don't say that out loud. Now, flip it into something positive, like: "My child sure does love his food! I know exactly what he's eaten. I get to teach him how to have good manners and remember to use his napkin." Or, flip the thought with gratefulness: "I'm so glad my child takes time to appreciate his food. Thank you, Lord, for using my child as an example of how to enjoy the little things in life like eating." The last step is to take these new, powerful, and encouraging flipped thoughts and share them.
>
> "Son, I love how you enjoy your food so much! It makes me want to enjoy mine more, too!"

Flipping those thoughts, at first, will seem really weird. You may feel like you're being mushy or insincere. For those of us who are used to being critical, it's a very difficult transformation but so very worth it for your family.

> **MACY: Encouragement comes most often through words.** For a long time, I believed I felt love most when people encouraged me. My best friends and I had journals in which

we'd write letters to each other every day during school. The first portion of the letters told about our day, our current crush, school drama, and anything we were struggling with. The majority of the note was saying all the things we liked about each other. We complimented each other for pages and pages on end. We thought that's what best friends did; it seemed simple to us. I loved reading my letters, and I felt loved when I heard all of the things my best friend loved about me. Words are powerful and they affected my attitude for a long time. They used to make or break my whole day, and sometimes they still can. They're powerful because words speak identity, and they help us define things. They're important, and families need to be aware of how powerful words are.

Let me offer you a few practical, applicable—most importantly, doable—tips on turning over a new leaf of encouragement in your home.

**Speak life.** Ephesians 4:29 says, *"Do not let any unwholesome talk come out of your mouths, but only what is helpful for building others up according to their needs, that it may benefit those who listen."*

That's a great standard to live by with your family. If it's not going to build them up, then don't say it! On the other hand, look for things to say that will build them up. This one was really hard for me to learn because I felt like my family would think I was insincere. I thought they would think I was throwing fluff at them. Not the case! As I've taken this verse to heart, my family now receives my "wholesome talk" as the encouragement that I mean to deliver.

**SUZANNE: Moms, quit telling your little girls they look ugly. Now I know you would never say, "You look ugly." But when you say, "Your hair is a mess," or "Your dress is filthy," or "That doesn't match at all," or ask "When was the last time you took a shower?" what they're hearing is, "Mom thinks I'm ugly." Remember, we want to fill them with courage, build them up, and speak things that benefit.**

So, a better way to encourage good hygiene is to say, "Before we leave, will you brush your hair and make it all beautiful and shiny? I'm so glad you had such a good day in your dress. Look at all this fun you've had! I think next time you wear that shirt; navy bottoms would look great!" Get the picture? Need one more example? Here you go. "Let's make it a point to brush our teeth! I love it when your teeth are white and sparkly."

Everything we say and do should be life-giving, even when it's direction and correction. We can and will honor our kids with the way we use our words.

**Be specific.** It's great to say, "Good job!" It's better to say, "You were a really big help on that project today! I was impressed with how hard you worked!" See the difference? The more specific you can be, the better your encouragement will be received.

*We can and will honor our kids with the way we use our words.*

**Encourage character, not outcome.** In youth sports, for example, we don't control the quality of our opponent. Therefore, praising wins and criticizing losses is an ineffective way to encourage. Did he do his best? Did she hustle? Is he improving? Find something in her game you can encourage. Curb pointing out all the things done wrong. If your child talks about all the things he did wrong in the game, don't participate in the pity party. Encourage. Build up. Especially right after the game when emotions are high for everyone. Leave the instruction for practice.

**Make a big deal out of it.** I have a friend who is a great encourager. I've learned a lot from him. I remember one time my youngest daughter McKenzie had a performance at church. When she came out, I said, "Good job, McKenzie!" That was pretty good, right? Well, my friend came up to her right afterwards and said, "McKenzie, that was amazing! You guys sounded great, and I loved the energy! It's obvious you worked really hard on that performance. Bravo!" McKenzie was beaming! I felt like a wet noodle. But I learned something: my kids like it a lot when I'm proud of them *and* excited about it.

**Encourage them even when they make fun of you for it.** It's funny. Most of us have no idea how to take a compliment. It hits our insecurities, and our first instinct is to deflect it because we don't think we're worth it. This can cause interesting reactions to your encouragement, some of which may be discouraging to you. Press on, my friend, because underneath the making fun of you they really like it!

**Pick your spots to correct.** This is important. Many people think being encouraging takes the rod of instruction out of our hands. Nothing could be further from the truth.

It's not that we never correct or rebuke our kids. We just need to pick our spots wisely; really think and pray about it before we open our mouths. The Word says, "*Preach the word; be prepared in season and out of season; correct, rebuke, and encourage—with great patience and careful instruction*" (2 Timothy 4:2).

I learned a great lesson from a friend of mine. Before he gets onto his kids about anything serious, he prays about it and then discusses it with his wife. That's wisdom. He'll tell you sometimes, after hearing from the Lord and his wife, he doesn't even go forward with the correction. But if he does, he handles it much better, and it goes much smoother. The parent who is careful with correction will find it's better received.

A quick note: Notice I used the word *correction*, just like in 2

Timothy 4:2, and did not use the word *criticism*. There is a difference. Criticism means to "judge unfavorably or harshly." Correction means "punishment intended to reform, improve, or rehabilitate." See the difference? Bringing unfavorable judgment on our kids doesn't do them any good. Our goal always needs to be not to judge and condemn, but to show them ways to improve.

Sometimes it's best to ask questions before we correct. When McCade was six years old, he came to me and said, "Dad, I'm allergic to corny dogs unless they have ketchup on them." Of course, my first response wanted to be, "That doesn't make any sense." Instead, I said, "Tell me more about that." McCade said, "When I eat corny dogs without ketchup, they make me want to throw up. But when I eat them with ketchup, that doesn't happen." After listening to him, rather than arguing with or correcting him, I realized in his six-year-old mind, he was right. He was allergic to corny dogs if they didn't have ketchup on them.

McCade came back about five minutes later and said, "Dad, those corny dogs without ketchup don't just make me *want* to throw up... We didn't have any ketchup, so I *just threw them up* in the bathroom." I jokingly said, "Go tell your mother. I need to write this down for a book illustration." Some things are just better left not corrected at all.

Second Timothy 4:2 says we are to correct with *"great patience and careful instruction."* By taking steps like asking questions, praying about it, and seeking counsel before correcting, you'll avoid a lot of unnecessary damage to hearts.

Of all the things we cover in our Crazy Cool Family ministry, becoming a person who encourages extravagantly and criticizes carefully is right at the top the list. As Hebrews 3:13 declares, encouragement changes hearts. It's especially true within your family. Encouragement will open up their hearts to you. It will open up their hearts to God. And it opens up their willingness to hear you and to be receptive to your counsel.

Encouragement makes everyone feel good. People like being around an encouraging person much more than a critical one. Don't you?

## safe

/sāf/

*adjective*

protected from or not exposed to danger or risk; not likely to be harmed or lost

*"Love begins at home, and it is not how much we do . . . but how much love we put in that action."*

—Mother Teresa

*My dear brothers and sisters, take note of this: Everyone should be quick to listen, slow to speak, and slow to become angry, because human anger does not produce the righteousness that God desires.*

—James 1:19-20

# Create Culture

| Encourage | Safe | Disciple | Unity |
|-----------|------|----------|-------|

# 10

## SAFE HAVEN

We always encourage our kids to bring their friends to our house—it keeps our kids home more, and we love hanging out with them and getting to know their friends. As you can imagine, we have kids of all ages and all types at the house, all the time.

Our kids will tell you, many of their friends are blown away by the openness in our home. We may have a boyfriend over, a group of teenage girls, or both, and they pretty consistently shake their heads in amazement at what our kids share with us and what we are willing to say and share with them.

When kids bring up something that troubles them, Suzanne will ask, "Have you talked about that with your parents?" The response is almost always, "Oh no! I would never do that!" It's not that they don't want to share it.

*Every kid longs to have an open relationship with his parents.*

It's that they feel sharing it with their parents is more costly than beneficial.

Let me let you in on a secret: Every kid longs to have an open relationship with his parents. They all wish they had parents they could count on to really listen to them.

Can you remember when you were a child or a teenager? Did you have parents where conversations had a cost, or was it beneficial? Are you the kind of parent you wanted your parents to be like?

We have the power as parents to create an open relationship culture in our home, and let me tell you, it is another game changer in creating a Crazy Cool Family.

Suzanne and I believe this openness is an absolutely critical component in our family and yours. We also believe any family can do it. Your family can do it. We call it creating a safe haven. Here's the CCC:

> CRAZY COOL PARENTS CREATE A SAFE HAVEN
> IN THEIR HOME WHERE THEIR CHILDREN CAN
> SHARE FREELY ABOUT THEIR LIVES.

## How Open is Open?

Let Mollie give you a picture.

**MOLLIE: Growing up, and even to this day, our house is known among our friends as the house where anything can be talked about. From topics like how bad our day was, to sex, to bodily functions, to speaking in tongues, to bad dreams, to fights with boyfriends—the list goes on. I have millions of examples, but I want to give one that blows people's minds and, at the same time, is such a true testament of how open our family is—and how it leads to fruitful connections with the Lord and each other.**

**My husband, Damian, was about to propose. Along the way, while he got to know my family, he and my dad pursued a sort of discipleship-type relationship. They met**

once a month and talked about life, about me, and about how to be a godly man in general. When Damian had THE meeting with Dad about marrying me, my dad spent more time discussing how much of a success he wanted Damian and me to be when it comes to sex than he did asking the usual Father-of-the-Bride questions. I can guess what you're thinking: (1) TMI! Too much information, Mollie, and (2) I can't even fathom a dad having THAT conversation with a man hoping to marry his daughter.

In answer to your first concern, understand there's no such thing as TMI with the Mannings. And if you can't fathom the example, that's precisely why I chose it!

When Damian told me, I wasn't surprised at all. I knew it because of countless conversations I had with my parents. They were willing to share their failures and successes in this area of marriage so Damian and I could walk into marriage prepared. You're probably wondering, "How is it Damian didn't run the other way?" My sweet fiancé knew, from day one, the openness of our family. He'd been at countless family dinners or hang outs that included some type of sex joke along the way, someone in tears about a relationship, or someone's deep spiritual journey with the Lord. He embraced the TMI Manning nature!

I got to walk into marriage a success in many areas because of my parents and the open dialogue at our house. And I got to walk into marriage a success in an area where many couples struggle because my parents laid a foundation of trust and openness that allows for deep-rooted heart connections. In this case, it just so happened to be about sex!

I really did have that conversation with Damian. Why? Because it's important! Do we want our kids to wait all their young adult lives to have sex and then have it be horrible for them the rest of their lives? That would be terrible! I want my children to be pure as they go into marriage, and then enjoy the benefits of that purity in their married lives. Suzanne and I are not going to leave such an important topic to chance, even if the fiancé does squirm a little bit. I'll confess, it was actually pretty funny to watch.

Creating a safe haven needs to be a purposeful endeavor. At times it's a little scary, but it's huge in creating a culture that builds your child's trust in the Lord and in their parents.

When we talk about a safe haven, we aren't talking about one in which our kids are protected from the dangers of life. When we talk about safe, we mean creating a place where our children trust us enough to be vulnerable with us. It's the place all of us, parents and children, desire. We want them to come to us with their ups and downs so we can have a deep relationship with them and help them navigate their journey. We know we've been through many of the same things they're going through.

Maybe you're frustrated as you read this. Despite your best efforts, you're discouraged about your relationship with your children as they get older. Maybe it feels like the harder you try to reach them, the more you push them away and the more distant they become. You're not alone. So many parents express those feelings to us. And as I've shared, I was there, too. I know the feeling, the fear, the frustration.

We often hear things like, "I try so hard to get my kids to talk to me, but it just doesn't work," and, "I ask them question after question, but they just give me one-word answers," or, "All they want to do is hang out with their friends or go to their room and get on their electronics with their friends."

The thing is, those parents are absolutely correct. Their children *are* avoiding them. They feel a comfort level with their friends that they don't feel with their parents. Why is that?

**SUZANNE: I hear from teenagers all the time the reason they don't share stuff with their parents is because they've seen their parents freak out, yell, scream, not let them talk anymore, judge, punish, control, or be overcome with fear, so much so that it damaged the trust the child had with the parent. In their minds, they deemed their parents as unsafe. It's just not worth it to go through all that drama,**

**so they would rather avoid, hide, or lie. Honestly, I wouldn't share my troubles, mess ups, or fears with anyone who reacted that way either. Why should we expect our kids to?**

What are the secrets to creating a safe haven culture where our children enjoy their parents and siblings and are willing to share life with us?

Creating a safe haven in our home begins with what we considered in the last chapter; changing our belief systems to a faith-filled view of our home rather than a fear-based view. If we live in fear about how our kids will grow up, the natural reaction is to overreact and control when we hear things concerning to us. When we trust God has our family in His hands, we see the troubling revelations of our children as opportunities to work with God to flip their beliefs.

There are some very practical things we can do to achieve this. Let me give you a few tips.

## Listen, Listen, Listen

Creating a safe haven culture is primarily about the power of listening.

I can't tell you how many times this scenario has unfolded in our home: Suzanne and I put the younger boys to bed and settled into bed ourselves—maybe 10:30 or 11:00. I drifted off to sleep, woke up an hour or so later, and reached over to discover Suzanne's side of the bed was empty. After an initial unsettledness, my thoughts would clear. I know exactly where she is, smile, and roll over to go back to sleep.

Where is the place my wife has left our bed for? She's at the foot of another bed in our house. One of our daughters had come home from a night out with friends—maybe even the boyfriend—and Suzanne is sitting at the foot of the bed listening to our daughter download about the evening. Sometimes the conversation only takes a few minutes and is uneventful. Other times, there's a lot to process, and it takes hours. Sometimes it's one-on-one. Sometimes two or three are there. But just about every time a daughter comes home, Suzanne is there to give them an ear—and notice, I said an ear, not an earful.

What do they talk about? Everything and nothing. Honestly, when I'm in on these conversations as a dad, I can either get bored to death or feel like my head is spinning. It takes so many words, and the conversations jump around like a pogo stick. Details are endless and many of those details, in my opinion, don't need to be included. But I've learned that efficient conversation isn't the point. It's not

*If we want our kids to open up to us, we must listen.*

even desired, because the more they talk—anyone for that matter, this doesn't just apply to kids—the more we learn about them.

So, listen, listen, listen. Realize, windows for listening will almost always be inconvenient. We'll have to battle ourselves constantly to not just jump in and give advice. The time required will always be in direct opposition to the time we have. It could seem like a complete waste of time. That's all true. But it doesn't change the fact: If we want our kids to open up to us, we must listen.

Listening applies to all ages. Suzanne is one of the best listeners I know.

**SUZANNE: I would do an experiment with my infants. At around two months they would start to coo, and it's delightful! I would sit in front of their little faces and coo and wait for them to coo back. It was our first conversation. I have no idea what we were talking about—heaven maybe. I noticed even at this very young age if I walked away, they would stop cooing and the conversation would end.**

**I realized everyone wants to be heard. From a baby trying to get your attention to a rebellious teenager acting**

out, everyone wants to be noticed. They want to know someone, particularly a parent, is willing to take the time to listen to them, and that what they have to say is important.

My mom used to always say about children, "They're just little people." If we will see them as that and offer them the same honor and respect we offer the cashier at the bank or the neighbor down the street, then they'll feel and act like little people, not overlooked, ignored, or demanding children.

Listening is so powerful at all ages. In fact, when your kids are younger, you can train them to share with you as they get older. Here is a great CCC to consider:

> IF YOU LISTEN TO THEM WHEN THEY'RE FIVE, THEY'LL TALK TO YOU WHEN THEY ARE FIFTEEN.

It's so true! Their stories may not make sense, they may talk too much, and they may tell you things you're not the least bit interested in. But remember, those who listen, accept, and love them will capture their hearts. Do you want that person to be you or someone else? If we listen to them, we'll get first dibs on influencing their hearts.

SUZANNE: I'm so practical, so let me give you some tips on how to incorporate quality listening into your relationships:
1. Take time to get on eye level and face them and listen to them.
2. Don't let yourself be distracted with the things of this world. (I find myself checking my phone when McCade is talking to me, and let's face it, it's rude).
3. Turn off the radio in the car and let them be the audio. Time in the car with your children as a captive audience is a great time to create safe havens. Everyone is a little distracted looking around, so they can be vulnerable AND there's no escape when the conversation gets hard.

Did you catch that? It's so important. If we establish ourselves as safe, especially early on, then we will be the ones our kids come to talk to when they need an ear. God gives us first rights as parents. Our kids are hardwired to desire a relationship with us. It's only after there's damage from things said, or things not said, that the relationship gets messy. Yes, there's some natural pulling away toward independence as they get older, but most of our relationship tension and lack of safety is caused by criticism and sin barriers, not independence.

## Earn the Right to be Heard

As our children start to share their lives with us, our natural tendency is to want to fix their every issue. I know the tension: "Who knows better than their parents?" We do indeed know a lot, but we have to earn the right to speak into our children's lives. You may be thinking, "Earn the right? How about the fact that we pay for absolutely everything? Doesn't that buy us the right to say what needs to be said? How else are our kids going to learn right from wrong? From their peers? I don't think so!" Sound familiar?

It has got to be one of the most difficult things in the world to hold back our advice for our children. We love them so much. We want the best for them, and we know our advice can really help—if they'd only listen to us. But no matter how great our answers are and how much we know, the hardened heart of a child cannot and will not hear the wonderful counsel of their parents. We can be frustrated and fume about it all day long, but it won't change the fact that we must earn our way into our kids' hearts. We earn our way into their hearts when they see we can be trusted with their feelings. We must listen with no agenda other than listening.

Because I know my own tendencies to not listen well and to give advice too freely, I try to focus on asking questions, biting my tongue, until my kids *drag advice out of me*. Can I confess? It's really hard, and I fail a lot. But my kids know Dad is trying to value them, and I'm working to overcome my natural tendencies—I want to listen more and give advice less. They give me credit for trying. And I'm getting much better at it, over time. By the time my youngest, McCade, gets to be a teenager, maybe I'll be listening as well as my wife. Okay, probably not. But a guy can dream, right? My point is, we don't have to be perfect. Just work at listening without judgment.

**SUZANNE: I'd like to offer some tricks on earning the right to be heard.**

*First, choose to be interested in what they're saying.* Die to your own agenda of what should happen, and choose to patiently hear their perspective of the situation.

*Second, value them.* Recognize that your kids are fascinating creatures with very clever thoughts and

*We earn our way into their hearts when they see we can be trusted with their feelings.*

insights to offer, not immature kids who don't know anything. If Jesus, the Savior of the world, valued them... so should we. *"People were bringing little children to Jesus for him to place his hands on them, but the disciples rebuked them. When Jesus saw this, he was indignant. He said to them, 'Let the little children come to me, and do not hinder them, for the kingdom of God belongs to such as these'... And he took the children in his arms, placed his hands on them and blessed them"* (Mark 10:13-16).

*Third, if you feel you must give advice, ask permission.* If you think you have exactly the right thing to say that will bring life, light, and love, ask, "May I share my opinion?" or "Would you like to hear my thoughts?" If they say no, recognize you have some work to do in your relationship because they may not feel safe. Encourage your child by saying you believe they'll do the right thing and end the conversation. But if they say yes, then you have an open door to bless them with your wisdom and experience.

# Ask Questions

**SUZANNE: The best way I know how to be safe is to ask questions. Remember Adam and Eve in the garden (Genesis 3:8-13)? They had just eaten the forbidden fruit and made themselves some lovely leaf clothing; when God entered the scene, they hid. The Lord asked Adam, "Where are you? Who told you that you were naked? What have you done?" Now in my mind, Adam and Eve had just messed up the best living situation ever for them and for us! And omniscient, omnipresent, omnipotent God the Father pursued them with questions. Yes, He knows the answers, and most likely we know the answers when we ask our children, too.**

**The goal of asking questions is not to get to the answers, it's to get to the heart of the matter. It's self-discovery, for them to have an *ah-ha moment* of revelation into the situation. Asking our children questions is so valuable. It teaches them they're important, and we're trustworthy and safe.**

**So how do we ask good questions?**

*Be curious* – Don't ask questions like you're in a court of law, interrogating witnesses. Rather, ask questions based in truly wanting to hear the reasons behind thoughts and actions. Use inquisitive questions, not accusatory ones. They really are brilliant, creative beings. When we give ourselves the time to get to know what makes them tick, then it's very interesting what they have to say. This is a *flip-your-thinking* kind of thing—if you can truly become curious (eager to learn or know) about what your children are experiencing, then a whole new door of communication will be open to you.

McKenzie is an expert on question-asking. Here's her advice for you:

**McKENZIE: Questions are one of my favorite things! They show you truly care, and open the door for someone to**

think rather than just be told. My favorite compliment someone gave to me was as I ask people questions, my curiosity for their lives causes them to discover things about themselves.

BE THAT KIND OF PERSON! Curiosity leads to discovery. Questions create a safe environment, and an open-door relationship. When you're asking questions, don't focus on what you're going to say next, but engage in what the person is saying. Make eye contact (unless in the car). It's your job to understand your children. If you're always answering your own questions to them, how will you discover who God has made them to be?

Some safe questions my parents have asked me, and I ask others are, "What were the highs and lows of the day?" and "What is one thing you learned today?" and "What is God teaching you right now?"

Often in our culture, it's not natural to be asked and cared about. Give the person time and preparation for the questions you ask. Silence is a good thing. It means that person thinks. Be specific. Ask about certain people and situations. Avoid broad yes-and-no questions that can be answered with one word. Also, live by example. Ask about them without expecting them to ask about you. Also, as a couple, ask each other to practice creating a culture of curiosity among your entire family. The biggest thing is that you don't give up after the first try. As I said before, it's something you're training your family in, and it's worth it.

## No Judging and No Lectures

Want to shut your kids down? Start to lecture about what they're doing wrong. When children do something wrong, they usually know what they've done and already feel bad about it. If you come in and add fuel to the already raging fire of guilt, don't be surprised they can't wait to get to their bedrooms, to get away from you.

**SUZANNE: One of the best parenting tools I use is remembering how I wanted to be parented. I'm a little bit of a perfectionist, so as a child when I messed up, I felt terrible. I'd hide in my closet wanting to get away from my mistakes. I didn't need anyone else heaping judgment or lectures on me. Were you that way as a child, too? Is your kid beating themselves up enough for the both of you? If so, then know that and meet your child where they are in the middle of the mess without judgment and lectures.**

What happens when we have done something wrong and we go to God with it? Does He bring condemnation? Not at all. In the Bible, over and over, God shows forgiveness and compassion. I love what Jesus says to the prostitute as the Pharisees accusing her slink away. In John 8:10-11, He basically says (my paraphrase), "Has no one else condemned you? Then neither do I. Now go and sin no more." Can you even imagine how freeing His words were?

I'll never forget how my dad treated me when, as a senior in high school, I totaled my Camaro—totally my fault. I rode in the tow truck bringing it home. To add to my shame, as we pulled up, I saw my parents had friends over. Perfect! As I approached the front door, I dreaded going inside and telling him. To my surprise, when I brought him outside to show him the mangled car, he just said, "I'm so glad you're OK and no one was hurt." He knew the consequence of losing the car I loved was more than enough in that miserable situation. He didn't need to add to my misery with more shame.

A lecture is defined as a "long, tedious reprimand." Who wants that? How about a short, to the point, non-repetitive reprimand? Let's have more of those! Your children will thank you!

## Get Ready for What You'll Hear

**MACY: Fifth grade was hard for me. I don't remember why it was so hard, but it was. I was the oldest kid at home**

doing school. I did most of my schoolwork online or on my own. I think Mom had just had a baby or something... it happened often. Math on the computer went like this: I'd watch the lesson, do my homework, grade my homework, take the quiz, grade the quiz, and stick it all in my folder to show my mom. A few weeks into this process, the lessons got really confusing. I started copying my work from the answer key. This went on for the majority of the school year. I felt crazy conviction. I actually cried while I was cheating but continued to do it because I felt like I had no other option.

I remember walking into my parent's room with the entire folder of false work I finished. I honestly had no idea how they would react, but I hoped they would understand and see things my way. I beat myself up for an entire year and I just needed them to help me. I don't remember exactly what they said, but here is what I know:

1. They didn't yell at me.
2. They didn't give me disappointed, shocked looks.
3. They listened to everything I had to say (even all my excuses).

It really did make a difference when I told them about my mistake. They made me re-do all the work, but I remember leaving the room feeling heard, seen, and forgiven. They said something along the lines of "we're not mad, but we wish you would've just asked for help." They never dwelled on my mistake. They just forgave and helped me forgive myself.

I think it's so important for a child to know their parents are willing to hear the whole story, and love and accept them no matter what the mistake is. I needed to come clean about cheating. They helped me do that by being a safe place for me to go and open up.

The reason parents and kids don't talk—and the same can be said of husband and wife—is because one or both sides are fearful of what they're going to hear or say. As you create the safe haven culture and your kids actually start to talk to you, expect to hear some issues you may not be comfortable with.

How do you approach these difficult conversations? Suzanne suggests helping our kids find God in the situation. Let me let her explain.

**SUZANNE: When my children tell me something that is going wrong in their lives, it takes everything in me not to give them my quick, easy, experienced answer, wanting to fix everything. I've found they never listen to that counsel. It seemed like it put me against them, like my well-intended counsel made things worse instead of better. As I was hyperventilating over whatever bombshell they'd just dropped on me, I started to ask a simple question that applies every time: "Where do you think God is in this situation?" Suddenly they were talking to me, and in many cases even giving me back the same information I would have given them! To make it even better, they sensed I was on their side. It didn't feel to them like I was an adversary. They felt free to process their dilemma with me and didn't feel they were being lectured by a parent. That strategy is worthy of a CCC:**

> WHEN YOUR CHILD BRINGS YOU A PROBLEM, ASK THEM, "WHERE DO YOU THINK GOD IS IN THAT SITUATION?"

I have both seen this in action and used it myself. It works! The girls even do it to each other now and use it in working through things with their friends. Instead of lecturing or responding in fear, Suzanne's strategy reaches into our kids' hearts to process issues in a way that deepens her connection with them and deepens their connection with God. Win-win! Double bonus!

Think about it like this: Instead of being on the other side of a situation with our lecturing and showing our kids we have the answer and they don't, we get on their side of the problem with them and work together to help them hear what God is saying to them. We get the same result—sometimes better—and to the kid, we're on their team and not just telling them what to do.

Creating a safe haven in your home won't happen overnight. You'll have to be very intentional about it. Work at it. Listening is key. It's a heart changer, softening parents' and children's hearts towards one another. Far more important than our kids hearing how smart we are, creating a safe haven where every family member feels the freedom to share whatever is on their hearts, free of criticism and judgment, makes home... *home.*

## dis·ci·pline

/disəplən/

*noun*

the practice of training people to obey rules or a code of behavior, using punishment to correct disobedience

*"Remember that you are not called to produce successful, upwardly mobile, highly educated, athletically talented machines...Giving your children great opportunities is good; it is not, however, the goal of parenting. Christlikeness is. Above all, seek to raise children who look and act a lot like Jesus."*

—Chip Ingram

*Discipline your children, for in that there is hope; do not be a willing party to their death.*

—Proverbs 19:18

# Create Culture

| Encourage | Safe | Disciple | Unity |
|-----------|------|----------|-------|

# 11

---

## RELATIONAL DISCIPLINE

Many times, as people listen to us talk about being encouraging and creating a safe haven in the home, we see a puzzled look in parents' eyes as they try to reconcile how to get their kids to be obedient while being nice and encouraging. Almost always, a parent will come up to us at the end of our seminar and ask us about a particularly difficult situation with their child. "I know I'm supposed to be encouraging, but what if my child is throwing a huge fit? No matter how much I try to reason with them, it just doesn't work! They only listen to threats and punishment!"

Having a child with significant discipline issues is draining on a family. It takes so much energy to nurture a child who just doesn't want to go with the program. Often, the conflicts aren't minor, and tension in the home becomes so thick you could cut it with a knife.

Let's face it: Sometimes we must use our power to control our kids. For example, our three-year-old is running into the street. We run after them and yell at the top of our voice, "Stop!!!" in order to save their life. We use every ounce of our power to control a potentially damaging situation.

Or our teenager is making bad grades and not doing their homework, so we limit his social activities until he chooses to do the right things to bring up his grades. We're using our power as a parent to provide incentive for the proper behavior. They say, "The Bible says we are to discipline our children—you know, 'spare the rod, spoil the child!'" Indeed, it does. I love this Proverb: *"Do not withhold discipline from a child; if you punish with the rod, they will not die. Punish with the rod and save them from death"* (Proverbs 23:13-14).

So how does discipline fit into a Crazy Cool parenting approach? Is there a way to discipline effectively without damaging the relationship?

Yes! Discipline, just like everything else in this book, starts with relationship. We don't lower the standards for our kids by pursuing discipline this way. In fact, I'd argue our standards for our kids are higher than most parents I meet. We're not satisfied with just outward obedience. We want Jesus deep inside their hearts.

To get there, we don't relax our standards. Instead, through Scripture, God shows us a different approach to get to these standards. God doesn't use control to make us obey. He pursues us through relationship. His example with us as our Father should move us away from a control model to a relational model where we are careful to only use our control when it's really needed instead of consistently defaulting to it at the expense of relationship.

We call this approach Relational Discipline. Relational Discipline starts from the inside and works outward rather than always trying to control the outward behavior.

If we're consistently defaulting to outward control of their actions, they'll never learn to internally control these actions. This is a major problem with almost every parent we know. We lecture, we yell, we get frustrated, we spank, we take away privileges, we lecture, we yell, we get frustrated, we spank, we take away privileges. An endless cycle of us trying to find ways to make them do what's right and them not meeting our standards.

Relational Discipline changes our focus. What if we only use control when we absolutely have to? What if we allow our kids to make mistakes and then use those mistakes as opportunities to help them toward knowing Jesus? What if our goal is self-control, not parent-control? Here's a CCC for you:

> CRAZY COOL PARENTS REALIZE THE GOAL OF DISCIPLINE IS NOT TO CONTROL, BUT TO CREATE PATHWAYS OF SELF-CONTROL.

It's great to talk about building pathways of self-control, and we would all love to have kids who obeyed our every word. But just how, you may ask, do I make that happen? I tell my kids over and over what to do, and they still don't obey. I have to stay on them all the time or they won't do anything!

So how is staying on them working out for you? Do you like the atmosphere it creates in your home? Isn't it exhausting? Are you worried what will happen when they leave your nest, when they start school, or, if they're older, go off to college?

What if we could get you off the treadmill of always getting on them? Telling them what to do over and over and over again. Arguing. Yelling. Slamming doors. Grounding. Taking away their cell phone for the fourth time this month. Putting them in time out. Spanking again.

Honestly, I can't remember the last time I spanked my kids. Not that I'm against it. It was always a last resort anyway, but it has not been needed. We've never grounded any of our teenagers. I think we've taken a cell phone away once, and that was actually a mistake. We've been through five teenagers so far and have never given them a curfew.

Galatians 5:16 says, "So, I say, walk by the Spirit, and you will not gratify the desires of the flesh." The

*Kids who walk by the Spirit build pathways of self-control.*

key to getting off the treadmill is for your kids to *"walk by the Spirit."* Kids who walk by the Spirit build pathways of self-control. Using Relational Discipline along with the other teachings in this book teaches our kids to walk by the Spirit so they don't have to be controlled by their parents.

So, what does Relational Discipline look like? In summary, it means our motive in discipline is to do all we can to avoid controlling situations and instead get our kids to agree with what God would want for their lives. This is a tough concept for a lot of parents because it hits a lot of our fears of losing control and our kids being damaged in some physical, emotional, or spiritual measure.

We've found it's easier to show you how Relational Discipline works in real life situations. As you see these specific teachings and examples, we hope God will speak to you about releasing control and having faith your kids will love a discipline approach that shows belief in them and in God.

## Think Before You Act

Imagine you're at your neighbor's house eating dinner with your family, including your two-year-old son. Recipe for disaster, right? After the meal, the kids seem to be playing nicely—one of your neighbor's older children is "watching" your two-year-old. It's quiet, and in the back of your mind that concerns you just a little. You slide gracefully into the next room where they're playing and discover your two-year-old joyfully pouring shampoo out of a bottle onto the carpet. It's puddling on the ground in an ever-widening circle.

Horrified, angry, and embarrassed—imagine it, now—you rush over to your child, rip the bottle of shampoo out of his hands, and spank his hand three times. You shout, "What are you doing? Don't you know that will ruin the carpet?"

What do you think? Is that strong discipline? Or poor parenting?

Look at it from the child's perspective for a moment. First, your two-year-old didn't know pouring a bottle of shampoo on the carpet would ruin it, and that was never his intention. In fact, he still doesn't know the shampoo will ruin the carpet because it still hasn't been explained to him. He did it because he thought it would look really cool for the shampoo to come out a bottle and pool up on that carpet. And it was fun.

Then, suddenly, his world changed dramatically. Mommy or Daddy came out of nowhere, shouting and hitting him for something he thought was really cool. Had Mommy or Daddy happened into the room without reacting, he probably would have smiled proudly and wanted to show off his shampoo creation.

So, what to do? Do you give the child a big hug and praise him for his creativity? Uh, no. But this story sets up a CCC:

> CRAZY COOL PARENTS ALWAYS
> THINK BEFORE THEY DISCIPLINE.

When you react in discipline situations, you'll almost always get it wrong. Even in this simple example, there are so many things at work and so many things we can understand about ourselves as parents and our child.

What was the intent of the child? Was the child intentionally doing something disobedient or just exploring life? Some have distinguished these behaviors referring to foolishness (intent to disobey) or childishness (exploring life).

Thinking through the child's intent gives us insight into the best response. What are his eyes telling you? Is there wonder in those eyes or deception? Did he keep pouring the shampoo on the carpet when you came in—assuming you came in calmly—or did he try to hide it?

Let's assume, like almost all two-year-olds in this situation, he was merely doing something he thought was fun. Our reaction should be to first remove whatever is doing the damage—in this case the shampoo bottle. Without freaking out, we need to show him that this is a mess, and messes are yucky. Why are they yucky? Because we have to clean them up.

Then the discipline comes in. We don't discipline this

situation by yelling and spanking him. We show him what a mess this is by having him help clean it up. Now, a two-year-old's clean-up skills aren't going to be great. But almost always, they'll tire of this game very quickly, especially as they see other kids doing fun things while they're stuck with you, wiping up shampoo. We work with them to stay with the clean-up until it's done. Cleaning up the mess teaches the child why pouring shampoo on the carpet isn't a good idea.

Children do, at times, deliberately disobey our instructions. They weigh the consequences, decide to take the chance, and choose foolishness to see if they can get away with it. When our oldest daughter, Mollie, was in her early teenage years, it was at the dawn of the social media revolution. There was a website called MySpace, a forerunner of Facebook, Twitter, and all of the current social media sites. Mollie really wanted to have a page on MySpace. She made a strong and consistent sales pitch on the many benefits of MySpace for her life—and mine, for that matter.

I decided to treat it as an opportunity for her to learn about technology and to see how she would respond in a challenging situation. I told her my primary concern about MySpace was she could potentially be exposing herself to bad people in the world. I was fine with her MySpacing with friends, but I had no intention of allowing people I didn't know to have access to her account. I told her I could do some research myself and configure safety and privacy features for her, but instead I wanted her to figure it out and show me how she could use MySpace safely. I said if she couldn't figure it out, come ask for my help.

A few weeks passed. I figured it wasn't that important to her because I didn't hear about it again. I should have known something was up because she went from talking about it every day to not talking about it at all—certainly not the first time I've missed something obvious in parenting. One day I was on our home computer—this was back in the days when we only had one, before iPads and smartphones—and I noticed a link in the history to a MySpace page. I clicked the link and, sure enough, there was Mollie's MySpace page she had created.

The privacy issue was more than she could handle, and I guess Dad was too scary, so she made a conscious decision to disregard my clear instructions.

I called her down to the computer and showed her the MySpace page I'd discovered, complete with pictures of her, her family, even including a silly picture of me. I asked, "Mollie, where did this MySpace page come from?"

"Oh, my friend Rachel created it for me and put stuff on it," she said. "Really?" I asked. "So, Rachel made this comment about the silly picture of me right here? I wouldn't think she would say that. Seems like that would have come from you." "Well maybe I added that one, but Rachel did the rest."

I asked Mollie to go get me the phone—back in the days we all used home phones. I told her I wanted to call Rachel so we could verify this was all her doing. At that point, tears started flowing. I'm not sure if her tears were the result of guilt or because she got caught, but it really didn't matter. This was a situation—fortunately for us not a common one—where Mollie had deliberately gone against my wishes. I was really angry, so angry in fact that as she started her "I'm so... so... so sorry" routine, I told her to leave me alone until I was ready to talk with her. In that moment, anything I said would have been a reaction out of anger, and I'd regret it later. Better to send her away until I gathered myself.

In this case, Mollie's intent was clear. She had willfully disobeyed me. This situation demanded a very firm response from me as the parent. Her actions had to have a consequence. What's funny about it, in hindsight, is I showed her the way to solve the privacy concerns I previously had in about five minutes. In other words, she had her MySpace page easily within reach, but her fear and lack of belief in her dad made her go the other direction, to sneak behind my back. She lost computer privileges for some time as the consequence.

Even in the times like this of deliberate disobedience, we still need to think about Relational Discipline. I asked questions to let her incriminate herself, so she was her own bad guy rather than me. I sent her to her room so I would not lash out at her and damage the relationship. Consequences could then be severe (and appropriate) without damaging the relationship. When times of harsh discipline come—and they will—we must be extra careful to think before we act.

Here's an example that might make you think a little: Some friends dealt with a situation where a group of teenage kids confessed to getting drunk after raiding one of the parents' liquor cabinets. One of the moms called Suzanne for advice. She told Suzanne how hurt and embarrassed and angry she was. How could her son do this to her? She just wanted to yell and scream at him.

Try to see it from your child's perspective.

Suzanne's response was not what she expected. She asked the mom this question: "Would you rather this happened to him while he's under your roof or when he goes away to college?" What if she looked at it as an opportunity to grow in her relationship with her son and to teach him the dangers of alcohol, underage drinking, and going against authority? What if, Suzanne counseled, the mom asked inquisitive and non-accusatory questions to try to find out what was going on in his head. Not by screaming, "What were you thinking?!?" But rather calmly asking and really wanting to know, "What were you thinking?"

"What was the appeal of that for you? Did you just want to see what it felt like? Did you want to escape something? Did you feel like you would be made fun of if you said no?" Try to see it from your child's perspective.

They're vulnerable at this point and expect the hammer to come down. If you'll get past your fears of their certain demise and start exploring the opportunity presented by this adversity, many times breakthrough happens for the child's relationship with God and your relationship with the child.

Adversity is this awesome opportunity to help your child see God, and you, from a whole new perspective. I like to tell parents this CCC:

> **THE DISCIPLINE HAMMER IS ALWAYS IN YOUR TOOLBOX. LEAVE IT THERE UNTIL IT'S THE RIGHT TIME TO USE IT!**

If you immediately start swinging, you may hit your mark, but you may also bust up some things you don't mean to bust up!

When we can take some time and initiative to think before we discipline, we will make huge strides in connecting with our kids relationally through our discipline.

There's always time to bring on the consequences. You have the consequences with you all the time. You are the parent. You have the power—which leads us to our next topic.

## Examine the Natural Consequences of Their Disobedience

It's best to consider what natural consequences our kids will face before we hand down our punishment. If the natural consequences of their misbehavior will be enough to teach them a lesson, then we can more easily move over to their side and help them work through it.

Remember the hammer analogy. You can always bring it out if needed, but first see if the natural consequences will work to change the behavior. Then you can be the good guy while discipline is still happening. Win-win!

**SUZANNE: One of my favorite comments to our kids is, "Oh, I hate that for you!" I say it when life deals them a consequence for something they didn't handle well—a toy they broke because they were too rough, a bad grade on a test they didn't prepare for, relationship issues, and so on. It's a great way of saying to them I believe consequences should happen, but nevertheless, I'm on their side with compassion to help them get through it. The discipline still occurs in their life, but now from their perspective I'm safe to them and on their side. There will be plenty of situations**

where I have to be the bad guy. But when life does it for them, I take advantage of those opportunities. I LOVE natural consequences! It's real world stuff! And that's what we're training them to do! Life out there in the big world.

> CRAZY COOL PARENTS CONSIDER THE NATURAL CONSEQUENCES BEFORE DISCIPLINING.

Our youngest, McCade, must have his notebook signed by a parent every school day. If he doesn't get it signed, then he has to walk five minutes at recess. It's an embarrassing punishment because all the other kids see him walk around the playground while they are having a great time.

He has forgotten a couple of times. Now Suzanne works at the school, and she could have run down there and rescued him. Instead, she let him walk—yes, a little embarrassing but a good natural consequence—and then she got to be sad with him and ask him how it felt, if he was embarrassed, mad at the teacher, or even mad at himself. In other words, she allowed a safe place for him to fail.

*"Oh, I hate that for you!"*

Guess what? He gets his book signed every night now. No more walking at recess for him. The natural consequences did their job!

## Consequences Need to Match the Offense

**SUZANNE:** I have a friend who takes her daughter's bedroom door off the hinges every time she does something wrong, like make a bad grade or talk rude to her little sister or not do her homework. Taking the door off the hinges is a brilliant and creative consequence, but not for those kinds of offenses. However, it's great for a child who is lacking self-control and continues to slam the bedroom door. Or for the child who is sneaky or inappropriate in order to earn the privilege of privacy.

I hear all the time about parents taking their kid's cell phone away for all kinds of offenses. I understand why. It's painful and easy. But when I talk to students whose parents constantly take their phones away for every offense, they have no respect for the discipline. They roll their eyes and say, "I don't have my cell phone again, but my parents will give it back as soon as they want to get in touch with me." It's a disconnected way to train a child. Now there are some very good reasons to take the phone away. If the child breaks rules about the appropriate times and uses of their phones—goes past a curfew, uses their phone inappropriately, looking at bad stuff, using social media irresponsibly, playing on the phone instead of doing chores or homework—a phone restriction may be appropriate. But don't take it away because they didn't feed the dog.

Our goal is to train our children to function successfully and to be a contributor to society. One of the best ways to do that is to show them how their actions create real consequences. When they speed, they get a ticket. The police officer doesn't take their phone away. If they steal, they go to jail. If they don't go to work, they get fired. These are real-life consequences. When you match the offense to the consequence, then real learning and self-control occurs. And if you can tie the whole situation to a future grown-up offense/consequence, then learning happens on a whole new level.

Here are a few consequences that match the offense— tied into our grown-up world.

If they don't do their homework, their consequence is to go to the teacher, apologize, and turn the work in, even if they don't get credit. Because in the future, if they don't do their job they'll have to talk to their boss.

If they're rude or mean to their siblings, they apologize and invest an hour doing whatever the sibling wants to do.

Because in the future, if they're rude and mean to customers they'll have to work to repair those relationships.

When a little kid throws his food on the floor, or pees in his pants, or makes a mess, his consequence is to be trained on how to clean up after himself. Because everyone needs to know how to clean up after themselves—especially when they make a mess—like when the trashcan falls over in the street and the trash goes everywhere. The homeowner is the one who picks it all up.

All this is directed by you, using a cool, calm voice, knowing you're investing in your child's future.

## See Things Through the Eyes of a Child

In one of his many books, John Maxwell shared about an opportunity he had to sit in a Q&A session with the late Rev. Paul Rees at a Leadership Conference. Rees, known for his insight and wisdom, was in his eighties at the time. Maxwell recalls: "Someone asked, 'If you could go back in your life and do something different, what would it be?' I'll never forget his reply. He answered, 'If I could go back to my days as a young father, I would work harder on seeing things through my children's eyes.' He went on to explain that he had missed many teaching moments because he wanted his children to see what he saw first. That day I made a commitment to see through the eyes of others before I asked them to see from my perspective."

SUZANNE: When Madeline was a baby, she was so fussy. I guess you could say she had colic. Needless to say, it was a stressful few months at the Manning house. Mollie was four and a half and didn't know how to handle this crying blob along with two stressed-out parents. Life had been all about her and so peaceful up until this new addition.

When we would go somewhere, Mollie would never want to leave even to the point of throwing a fit. As a stressed-out young parent, I didn't handle the situation well—let's just say Mollie was not the only one throwing a fit. That evening as I put Mollie to bed, I apologized for being a brat and then asked her why she made it so difficult to leave places. She simply said, "Because I don't want to come home." And then I saw life through her little-girl eyes. Life at home was not fun. It was scary, unsafe, and confusing. (I wanted to throw a fit when it was time to leave peaceful places to come home, too!) Seeing the situation from her perspective changed the way we handled the environment in our home and the way we prepared her to leave places. It was very eye-opening and valuable. Little kids are really smart, and their perspective is enlightening.

This topic relates to thinking before we discipline, but I think this point is worth highlighting separately. When you see things through the eyes of the child, it can change your whole perspective on the situation at hand. For one, we don't think about ourselves. Second, we can better discern our child's intent. And finally, it gets us to slow down and not make a relationship mistake that will cost us down the road.

Are you starting to see a pattern? Threaded through all these topics is our Relational Discipline approach. Yes, their behavior is important, but the relationship is so much more important. One, because great relationships are a lot more fun than bad ones, but also because our strong relationship with the child will lead them toward the behavior that is needed.

## Don't Let Embarrassment Drive Harshness

Back to our two-year-old example. Here's another CCC:

> OUR KIDS WILL EMBARRASS US SOMETIMES.
> CRAZY COOL PARENTS DON'T LET
> EMBARRASSMENT LEAD TO OVERREACTION.

Let me tell you something about embarrassment as a parent: It's going to happen. Depending on your standards, it may happen a lot. Overreaction to your embarrassment is a recipe for discipline disaster.

If you don't have thick enough skin to survive being embarrassed by your kids from time to time, then don't have them. Otherwise, get over it! When your children embarrass you, you cannot let it become more about your embarrassment than about the right and appropriate discipline for your kids. Embarrassed, angry parents who are so concerned about their image do more harm to their kids than they realize. Maybe you know someone who has grown up in an environment like that. They tend to develop a sense of shame because they could seemingly never do anything right for Mom and Dad. This is one of those negative relationship issues that wounds a child and will stay with them.

> **SUZANNE: I watched this scene unfold in a restaurant. A three-year-old little boy was running around and spilled his drink. He was devastated and started crying and making a scene. The embarrassed mother quickly got up, jerked the child back to their booth, told him to be quiet, and then went to clean up the spilled mess, the whole time glaring at her distraught son. Imagine that same scene, but this time the mom quietly communicates with her son, telling him she's so sorry he spilled his drink, and that usually happens when we run with beverages in our hands. Then she channels all that devastated emotion into having him help her clean up the mess, and then shows him how walking is way better than running in a restaurant especially with a drink. That's an opportunity to take a bad scene and train your child how to successfully manage it.**

If I were to have a heart-to-heart talk with parents on this issue, they'd tell me without a doubt, never in their wildest nightmare do they want to develop a heart filled with shame and fear in their child. Parents don't set out intending to cause damage to their children. It's either they don't understand the consequences of their actions or they're struggling to overcome their own issues which lead to this behavior. Once their actions are brought into the light, they better understand how to heal their own hearts and begin the work of shaping the hearts of their children as well.

The first thing we must recognize is when our feelings are getting the best of us. Sometimes we don't even know that we're acting out of embarrassment. As we learn to stop reacting first and put our parenting before the Lord, God will start to show us the source of our behavior. Ask yourself: Am I doing what I'm doing in the best interest of my child or because I'm upset? Is what I'm doing going to speak life and hope into my child or become a source of bitterness for her? Am I venting or looking out for my child?

## Life Is in the Why

*Our children get far more than we realize.*

Children understand far more than they communicate at every age. When my oldest daughter, Mollie, was one year old, she couldn't say much to us. I thought she understood about as much as she talked. I soon learned from my wife I was very wrong. She would say to Mollie, "Go get your red shoes out of the closet and bring them to me." Mollie would stand there for a few seconds—which seemed like an eternity to me—while she processed this instruction. Then, off she would go to find the red shoes in the closet! She couldn't say the words, but she could understand them.

Our children get far more than we realize. Even when they don't acknowledge understanding, it's being deposited in their little brains. They're taking it in and evaluating it according to the grid that's already established at that point.

Therefore, it's so important our children understand why we're disciplining them. It doesn't mean they have to agree. We're not running a popularity contest here. Some subjects can't be up for debate. It is our responsibility, however, to communicate. We can even let them know it pains us to have to discipline them. I don't know any parents who are so spiteful they enjoy discipline. Good grief! I wouldn't want to know those parents! Giving yourself the requirement of communicating with your child about the discipline will help mitigate your anger. It's hard to communicate clearly when our head is clouded with anger and frustration.

**SUZANNE: This can become a sticky situation for some parents because their children whine and complain, expecting an explanation for everything. You've heard it— or said it—before, the parent gets exhausted and blurts out the famous parental line, "Because I said so!" While that statement is true—we're the parent, we're in control, we're the authority—when we don't explain the *why*, it does nothing to build the child's wisdom and understanding.**

**Think about the stage a three-year-old goes through, where they ask *why* about everything, to the point of annoyance. What they're really doing is building a database of information on how to do life successfully on this earth. By the time they're in elementary or a teenage, the needs for input into the database change dramatically. But now they don't know how to ask the *why* innocently like the three- year-old. They either don't ask and act like they know it all or ask with a sassy tone that makes you want to shut them down.**

**Imagine kids as a giant whiteboard. The world, school, friends, media, church, and parents are all writing on this board. As parents, you want to write the *why* so the next time your kids are exposed to a situation in which they'll need to make a choice, they'll have the data to draw from to make the right one. We need to know our marker makes the boldest mark on that board. Our marks are the ones that point them to Jesus, help them navigate this world successfully, and empower them to be mighty men and women of God. That's *why* we explain the *why*.**

## Act Like the Parent, Not the Child

Discipline doesn't have to be—and shouldn't be—a war. So many times, we see a child throw a fit and then the parent throws an even bigger fit in disciplining the child! When a parent talks of being out of control with a child, my wife will remind them, "You're the parent! Act like it!" Hey, parents, you don't get to throw fits. It was tolerated as a child, but not as a Christian adult. The apostle Paul said, *"When I was a child, I talked like a child, I thought like a child, I reasoned like a child. When I became a man, I put the ways of childhood behind me"* (1 Corinthians 13:11). Children are learning self-control. How are they ever going to learn it if their parents can't model it? The parent who's calm and firm with an out-of-control child will win that child's heart in the long run.

So, what happens when we let our discipline get out of control? What if we spank a child in anger or yell and scream at them as we lose our self-control? Do we hope to do better next time or accept that we're just angry people? Perhaps we make it worse by blaming the child for our lack of self-control? "Well, I wouldn't get so mad if you'd just act right!" Is the child really responsible for our behavior? Of course not.

> **SUZANNE: Every one of my children have told me, now that they're older, they didn't like it when I was angry or threw a fit. They say it made them feel like things were out of control because the person in charge was acting out of control. Our children have no idea what to do when the adult in charge is acting like the child. They don't have the maturity to be the adult... that has to be us. Please learn from my kids and my mistakes. Choose self-control. Don't allow yourself to freak out on your child. Remove yourself from the situation before you cause any damage. Ask yourself, "What needs to happen so I'll react like an adult in this situation?"**

# Ask Forgiveness When You Mess Up

*"Forgiveness is me giving up my right to hurt you for hurting me."*

—Anonymous

When we lose our self-control in attempts to discipline our children, we should go back to them and ask their forgiveness for our wrong to them. No matter what their offense, we never have the right to blow up at them. Two wrongs don't make a right. We must understand that our anger and lack of self-control always causes damage in our children's hearts. Your parenting standard always needs to be that you maintain self-control at all times. We'll fail sometimes. But by understanding the harm our anger-filled discipline does, we work harder to remove it from our lives.

When it does happen, we can recover our relationship through asking forgiveness. I can't tell you how many times my children have done something that made me fly off the handle at them. After I calmed down, I realized my error and went to them to ask their forgiveness. Setting the standard of asking forgiveness actually helps me to avoid these situations because I don't want to put myself in them again. When my kids see Dad humbling himself to ask forgiveness, they see a dad who desires to tear down the walls the enemy wants to build through anger and lack of self-control.

Forgiveness and restoration are vitally important to parenting. Many think you have to be tough in order to discipline. We understand that mindset—we actually lived it for many years. We've also seen the opposite, parents catering to their kids' every whim. We knew that route led to spoiled, selfish kids, and doesn't bring joy and life into their homes.

Jesus showed us a different model; a Relational Discipline model. Do you remember, in John chapter 18, when Peter denied Jesus three times? Before it went down, Jesus had told him exactly what was going to happen—three times. Then it did, and Jesus saw it happen during one of Peter's most vulnerable moments. Later, after Jesus had gone to the cross and been resurrected, He found Peter fishing.

If our child had done something like that to us—deny us three times after we'd told them what was going to happen—I suspect we may have responded, "Peter! Get over here! Get out of that boat right now, young man. I need you on this beach, IMMEDIATELY! What were you thinking? Didn't I tell you what was coming? Didn't I warn you specifically about what would happen? I told you three times you were going to deny me and still you failed. I don't know what else to do. I mean, this is just another time when you have failed me. Even when I was arrested, I had already told you I was going to leave. I don't know what to say here. This is just another indication of repeated failure in your life!" Can you hear that lecture?

But Jesus took a totally different approach to parenting Peter. First of all, He sought him out. Jesus looked for Peter with the purpose of restoring him. When He found him, the story in John 21 says He made him breakfast and made sure he caught a lot of fish. I am sure, even though Peter was excited to see Jesus, he wasn't expecting what he received from his Lord. Jesus restored Peter. Jesus had prophesied over Peter that he would be the Rock on which Jesus would build His Church. Peter's mistakes hadn't changed that. Jesus understood mistakes are part of the maturing process, and Peter had already suffered under the natural consequences of his failure. Jesus didn't need to add to the damage sin had already done to Peter's heart.

Jesus restored him. He asked Peter, "Do you love me?" and told him to feed His sheep—three times, once for each denial. Jesus healed Peter's heart. The result? First, Pentecost. Then a disciple who, along with all the others, was accused of "turning the world upside down" for Jesus' sake.

Jesus didn't change the standard for Peter. He never said the denial was the right thing to do. He simply kept His self-control and made Peter understand that He was on his side. Jesus knew the natural consequences of Peter's actions were more than enough punishment. The time for hurt had passed, and the time for forgiveness and restoration was at hand.

# Think Disciple, Not Discipline

This is a great one to end on because it ties back to Jesus. Think of Jesus and His disciples. Jesus took a bunch of average men and turned them into spiritual superstars! How did He do it? He discipled them. He first modeled it and then He taught it with patience and grace.

Think about it. If anyone had the right to be fearful about his "kids," it was Jesus. He was about to hand over the most important mission in the world after only three years with these unschooled men. If they failed, it was only going to impact the history of the world. No big deal.

Yet Jesus didn't trust in them. He entrusted them to His Heavenly Father. He had faith what God wanted accomplished in their lives would be done. His belief led Him to not act out of fear, but out of faith. And these average men changed the world!

Now I don't know about you, but I think my kids are a little better than average. You may think that about yours as well. If we can disciple our above average kids with an above average faith, what might God do with their lives?

**SUZANNE: We get the crazy opportunity to disciple our children. Just like Jesus, we get to spend hours and hours with them showing them how to live in this world and still believe in a better world. We're the ones who get to fill them full of hope, and show them the commands of Christ and the examples of His love, grace and mercy. Like Jesus, we get to teach them about God's kingdom and His word and His purpose for their lives. As you read about how Jesus invested in His disciples, imagine yourself in that scene with your children: feeding the 5000, catching all the fish, walking on water. We get to teach our kids to walk on water! In other words, we get to teach them to do the impossible. To have enough faith to move mountains. We get to teach them about God's creation. Oh, the list goes on and on! It's a very high calling we as parents have to disciple our children!**

# Conclusions

What does discipline look like in the Manning home? It's definitely a work in progress. Suzanne and I are not always on the same page and many times we miss things or go overboard with our discipline actions. Certainly, the older sisters will tell you that life is so much easier for their younger brothers than it was for them. And they're right. In 20-plus years of parenting we've definitely learned some more efficient, graceful ways to parent. Somehow our older kids survived and thrived. But the best way to give you an idea of discipline at the Manning home is to ask the kids.

**MOLLIE: I think the biggest thing to note about discipline at our house was it was always done in love. I know parents say that to kids as the justification for discipline a lot of the times. But my parents hardly ever said it; they simply showed it. When we got in trouble or were disciplined there was rarely a trace of anger, more a trace of sadness. And as I'm older, I know that sadness was the realization that sin is bad, and evil, and as parents you have to watch your children grow into the sin that haunts the world. My parents rarely yelled at us, they didn't hit or spank when they were angry, regardless of how angry our actions actually made them. Their tone was firm, but understanding. As a child, I always knew they truly wanted what was best for me, because it showed in all areas of our lives.**

**MACY: Parents, please discipline your children. I've spent countless hours babysitting and it's clear who is disciplined and who is not. When our parents disciplined us, we knew what we did wrong, why it was wrong, and how we could adapt to make things right. Be honest with your children and let them in on the secrets of hard work, humility, and unconditional love. Tell them how their actions affect others and they're learning how to love God and love others right now! Discipline is biblical and necessary for**

young kids. They need guidance and training on how to be like Jesus. Discipline helps cultivate respect and honor, both of which parents deserve. You deserve to be obeyed and listened to by your kids. The authority has been given to you, by God. Use it with love and compassion and your kids will become more like Jesus. You're the disciple of your kids and you have a tremendous say in their character. Allow the Holy Spirit to work in you and through you every day as you raise up your children. God makes it possible, so trust in Him! Parents, please discipline your children.

I promise, we didn't coach our children to say that. It's not forced upon them to make us look good in the book. They

really believe what they're saying. I'll tell you something else: They don't realize it, but their memory is very favorable to us. Because over time, God taught us more and more how to discipline in love. We made a lot of discipline mistakes in our early years of parenting. Both Suzanne and I definitely had—and still have—our parenting flaws. However, it's amazing to me how our change toward God helped our children to forget our flaws. I think that is a great example of the grace of God.

*Parents, please discipline your children.*

SUZANNE: Children are to be a blessing to their parents, their family, their peers and the world. There's nothing more annoying than a child who lacks self-control. When we were young in our parenting we went to several conferences and at one of them they taught this proverb: *"A wise son brings joy to his father, but a foolish son brings grief to his mother"* (Proverbs 10:1). How they taught it really impacted the way I parented. They said as a mom it was my job to train my children to be wise because then they would be a joy to their father (and to me and the family too, of course). Did you catch it? If they were foolish they would grieve their mother because she gets the most time of the first and most important years of a child's life. She's the one to daily pour God's truth and wisdom into her children. I took that responsibility very seriously. I was the one on the front lines of teaching my sons and daughters how to be godly men and women. I tell newly married women who want to have several children the key to getting your husband on board is to train your children to be wise, to be a blessing! And who doesn't want more blessings right? But when your child is a brat, it stresses everyone out and they're not a joy. A well behaved, well adjusted, joyful child is a delight to be around. It's our responsibility as parents to build that kind of child.

As you can see our standards for our children are very high. With Relational Discipline, the standards don't change. The approach does. When we discipline from a relational perspective, we get the standards with the relationship and we get kids who live and obey from the heart, and not primarily out of control. Control only goes so far, but connecting them to Jesus and creating pathways of self-control goes into eternity.

## u·ni·ty

/yoo'nĭ-tē/

noun

1. The state or quality of being one or united into a whole
2. The state or quality of being in accord; harmony

*"A family doesn't need to be perfect. It just needs to be united."*
*—Anonymous*

*I have given them the glory that you gave me, that they may be one as we are one – I in them and you in me – so that they may be brought to complete unity. Then the world will know that you have sent me and have loved them even as you have loved me.*
*—John 17:22-23*

# Create Culture

| Encourage | Safe | Disciple | Unity |
|-----------|------|----------|-------|

# 12

---

## BUILDING UNITY

Psalm 133:1 says, *"How good and pleasant it is when God's people live together in unity!"* Throughout our world, God designed different things to come together and work in unity.

You want proof? Look at nature. Look at the uniqueness of the world God has created yet different parts come together to make life possible. Further proof? Look at our own bodies. The unique parts of our body come together in unity to form our physical person.

God intended for each member of our family to be different. To be unique. It wasn't an accident. He has a purpose for it. Yet the enemy uses these differences to bring about tremendous wounds and conflicts in our home. God has a different plan. He wants to show us how to use these very differences instead to bring blessings into our home and to deepen relationships instead of wounding them.

How do we do that? How do we make all the arrows in our home go in the same direction? We bring unity into our family. Let's define unity. First, here's what unity **does not** mean:

- Unity doesn't mean everyone agrees with everybody else

in every situation. There are things we need to agree on, certainly, but our family will never be in agreement with everything. There will always be different opinions. We need to prepare for that as parents.

- Unity isn't manipulative. We don't squash different opinions by guilting someone with the unity club. "You're being disloyal." That's not promoting unity. That's just condemnation and manipulation.
- Unity doesn't mean everyone looks and acts the same. Instead of trying to put everyone into the same mold, we'll bring out the uniqueness of each arrow as we move in the same direction.

Unity **does** mean this:

- The family, led by the parents, serves each other. Philippians 2:3-4 says, *"Do nothing out of selfish ambition or vain conceit. Rather, in humility value others above yourselves, not looking to your own interests but each of you to the interests of others."* We serve by example, and we call our kids to serve as well.
- The family promotes each other. We're excited about one another's successes, and we encourage each other in our difficulties. We look out for each other, and we take care of each other.
- The family loves each other. A unified family loves instead of judges. They forgive and overcome together.

When we talk to parents about unity, it's a broad concept that can take many forms. For clarity, we focus on three areas: Unity as parents, unity in siblings, and unity in family. We talked about unity in siblings earlier, remember Siblings as Best Friends? In this chapter, we'll focus on unity as parents and the family as a whole.

## Unity as Parents

As we talk to parents about the highs and lows of raising families, we hear recurring themes. Here are some we hear often:

- The problem with our kids is my wife. She lets them run all over her all day long and then expects me to discipline them when I come home.
- The problem with our kids is my husband. He's constantly picking at everything they do. If he would just back off, things would be much better. He's always so angry.
- My husband expects me to raise the kids alone. All he does is come home and sit on the couch and watch TV.
- My wife is so disorganized. I try to help her get our home organized and all we do is fight about it.

Any of that sound familiar? Early in our marriage and parenting adventure, we tended to focus on each other's differences in a negative way. Both Suzanne and I thought, "If only I could get my spouse to see things my way and do things the way I do. Then we'd be on the same team, and everything would work so much better!" That thinking led us to criticize one another in order to "help," and we became completely exasperated as each of us received it as condemning criticism.

In the same way we celebrate differences within our children, God showed us He created each of us uniquely as well. He's not at all surprised we got married. He wants us—and you—to believe that He brought us—and you—together as the best marriage team for our—and your—family. We shouldn't focus on making our spouse more like us, but rather making our spouse the best version he or she can be.

On this matter, Suzanne and I will both offer our own testimonies. We have both struggled to overcome the desire to change one another. Today, we're much better at celebrating our differences and seeing them as strengths rather than hindrances.

## Husbands, Get on Your Wife's Team

As you're reading this book, I'm sure you realize I married far better than I deserved. Really, Suzanne should be writing this book, not me. A lot of this material comes from her. Often, husbands look down on their wives' thoughts on parenting because she tends to be more relational and less systems-/ discipline-oriented. Husbands worry they're not tough enough on the kids, that they let too much slide.

I was absolutely on that train the first several years of my parenting life. As I watched my wife parent, I somewhat looked down my nose at her with a dose of exasperation. I never had any problems getting the girls to obey me. All I had to do was let them know I was serious, and it was over. Suzanne would negotiate with them and let them complain. "Honey," I'd say, "all you have to do is be a little firmer and they won't run all over you. It's not that hard."

If you have a wife who operates more on the relational side of parenting, there may indeed be a lack in firmness. But as we focus on the perceived flaw in their approach, we miss the wonderful ways they interact with our children, reaching their hearts in ways no discipline or system ever will. God made our wives more relational for a reason. He wants to take the best of both of us and blend it into a parenting team that's perfectly balanced.

Once I realized God had much to teach me through watching my wife parent our children, I discovered in her a treasure chest of lessons. I can't do it the same way she does because we're very different personalities, but there's so much to learn in how she interacts with them and draws them out. It's like watching Tom Brady carve up a defense or Clayton Kershaw pitch a baseball game—it's a thing of beauty.

Husbands, we have a lot to learn about relationships, and God gave us an in-house teacher in our wives. I envision wives, here, elbowing husbands, "See this! Don said..." But I absolutely want to

*He wants to take the best of both of us and blend it into a parenting team that's perfectly balanced.*

encourage husbands, be open to learning about this relationship business by watching your wife interact with your children. I've said it before, but it bears repeating: Husbands, if you'll become a student of your wife instead of her critic, you'll be amazed at what you will learn about your family!

Now from Suzanne...

## Wives, Get on Your Husband's Team

SUZANNE: Wives, can I be honest here? One of the hardest things in my marriage has been parenting on the same team as my husband. God has designed men and women to be very different and WOW! does it show up in our approach to parenting!

For years, I fought Don on how he interacted with our children, especially Mollie because I brought her into the marriage. Whatever Don would do, I'd argue. Sometimes it would even be in front of the children. Not good!

At one of the many parenting conferences we went to, my whole perspective on parenting with my husband changed. We were taught how to be on the same team, that our differences are a benefit, and to embrace them. I started seeing Don as an ally, instead of someone I had to overcome. I knew he wanted the best for our children, but I didn't believe or agree his methods were as good as mine. The reality of the situation was that, with only my influence, our children wouldn't be very hard-working or disciplined. Don has crazy perseverance and is constantly challenging the kids to give their best.

Don brings vision and direction to our family. He sees where our children and our family need to go, and he has a plan to get us there. While I parent in the moment, he looks ahead to the future. He works on values and character and inward obedience.

Once I realized we're a team and in this parenting journey together—that we both make mistakes, and we both have gifts our children need—then our parenting started exploding with success. I'd offer this insight: Wives, stop focusing on what your husband is doing wrong and embrace all your differences. Be on his team!

I hope you can see by our personal stories that getting on the same team is a process. First, you must have a change of belief—like Suzanne did at the parenting conference. Then it takes work and perseverance to implement the new belief into your daily parenting and family life. All of us like the way we do things, think we're right, and think others should do the same. But God made us different for a reason. In our families, He made us different to help our children become all He wants for them.

What does it look like for a married couple to be on the same team in parenting? It's hard to be exhaustive here since everyone is truly different. But here are some great things that apply to almost everyone to help you get on the same team.

## Learn from Your Spouse
## Before You Criticize

God gave you the perfect spouse for you to learn exactly what you need to know about parenting your children. Study your spouse as he or she interacts with your children. They love your kids as much as you do. They want what's best for them, too. Make sure you're catching what God is saying to you through your spouse about your family.

I've learned more from my wife about my children and how to parent them than any other single source. Period. Not even close. It took me about ten years to come to that realization. I hope you'll get it sooner than I did.

## Discuss Parenting Conflict
## Issues Privately

As much as possible, let it go. Do your best not to argue in front of your children about the way each of you handle a parenting situation. For starters, you're conveying a negative emotion which isn't good. Moreover, you're unwittingly encouraging the child to disregard the instruction of the parent who's not on his or her side. You've seen a child jump on the bandwagon of pitting one parent against the other—you don't want to be there. Take it up later if you must, in private.

I realize letting something go feels like the situation is being mishandled. Guess what? It's okay! There's always going to be another opportunity to parent. Just let it go, take the negative emotion to the Lord, and then later, have a calm conversation in private with your spouse about the issue.

Think of the benefits of employing this strategy. First, you'll gain major points with your spouse for honoring them even if they're wrong. No one likes to be corrected, especially not in an embarrassing way. Second, you'll minimize and hopefully eliminate your child's ability to play you against each other. They need to know there's no room for that in your home. Most important, it's best for your child. When you have an argument in front of your children about something they've done, they can feel guilty their actions are the source of conflict between Mom and Dad. This is a major reason kids feel it's their fault when their parents get divorced.

## Always Honor Your Spouse

If there's one thing I pray everyone who reads this book will absolutely take to heart, it's this: Never, never, NEVER talk bad about your spouse, anywhere, to anyone! And especially not in front of your children! I see men and women criticizing their spouses, joking about them, making themselves look good at their spouse's expense in so many situations. You've heard it, too: "It won't happen if it's up to my wife to do it!" "Yeah right! My husband fix something around the house? No chance!" "We would be on time if it weren't for my wife. She's always running late."

Please, hear me! Don't do it. Nothing good can come of it. Nothing!

It's counterproductive. Whether consciously or subconsciously, when we criticize our spouse, we're thinking it makes us look better. It doesn't. I lose respect for a person who is publicly critical of their spouse. I feel an empathy for the spouse and typically come away with a more favorable opinion of them than their critic. The critic looks petty and condescending—sort of like a Pharisee.

## Praise Your Spouse in Front of Your Kids

What if you went the other way? Instead of criticizing your spouse, what if you looked for good things and made it a point to praise those actions? My wife is especially good at this. She tells our kids all the time what a great father they have. From being a great provider, to investing in their lives, to not being angry with them all the time; she consistently finds my best points and shares them with my kids.

We've experienced the truth in this CCC:

> THE MORE YOU PRAISE YOUR SPOUSE, THE
> MORE YOUR KIDS WILL LOVE YOU!

It works! Children want unity in the home. It's a God-given desire, put into their hearts. When you're the one bringing unity into your home, telling your kids what a great mom or dad they have, you're being a unity agent in your home. Your kids will appreciate you more and more for being an agent of positive change.

We bring unity into our homes when we embrace the differences each spouse brings to the family. The whole family wins when you form a unified—unbeatable—parenting team.

## The Family Name

**SUZANNE: Unity in the family is a really big deal. It resonates with many of the families we teach. God put this unifying concept in my heart early in our family journey, and I've watched it grow in our lives.**

**If you want to know whether something has stuck within your family, listen to your kids talk about it with others when they don't know you're listening. With this concept,**

our children own it so deeply they talk about it with their siblings and others. When they're talking about it, you know it's gone beyond your own heart and into theirs—and it's so cool to see it happen!

I'm very grateful for the way my husband joins me in instilling this concept into our family. I don't take this for granted. We've seen, so often, parents who feel like they oppose each other, battling to get to what *they think* is right. We've seen others behave childishly—if the idea wasn't theirs, they won't join in. That's not the case with Don. He really doesn't care whose idea it is. In this case, he's a strong believer and a huge influence in getting this message across to our kids.

What's the amazing concept God laid on my heart? We call it *The Family Name*. A CCC for you:

> OUR FAMILY NAME UNITES US AND HELPS
> US TO SEE THAT LIFE IS BIGGER THAN US.

From an early age, we've instilled the pride and importance of being a Manning in our kids. Now it's not that we come from royalty or anything. It's not even about the particular name. It's about the family.

Our kids need to understand life is about more than just them. What better place to learn that concept than in the safe confines of home and family? The more we focus on pleasing ourselves, the less it actually happens. In God's economy, the more we focus on Him and others, the more He meets our needs and in greater measure than we could ever imagine.

Our kids need to understand when they help others, make good grades, achieve in sports or fine arts, say a kind word to someone, walk with integrity, or do anything else that brings honor to God and brings good into a situation, they're not only bringing honor to themselves and to God, but they're bringing honor and favor to the family as well. Each family member, over time, receives the benefit of those honorable tasks that were done.

On the other hand, when a parent or child says or does things that are dishonoring—rudeness, selfishness, laziness, etc.—it not only discredits their personal name and the name of the God they serve, but it also makes it more difficult for the other family members. It's an important life-lesson: Our actions have impact far beyond ourselves.

Some people have argued with us saying this puts pressure on the child. I disagree. The same parent will put their child on a select sports team and tell him or her how important it is to be a part of the team. Why is it important to be on a team? To learn life is about more than you. What better place to have a team than at home?

*Our kids need to understand life is about more than just them.*

When you couple the family name with the safe environment with siblings as best friends, it does wonders to keep sibling conflict to a minimum. It starts your kids down the path of pulling for each other instead of the petty jealousies that plague many families—and have since the beginning of families, for that matter. Just see the twelve sons of Israel as an example.

I'm amazed at how our older girls encourage and teach our younger boys. Part of it is a genuine love for them, but part of it is their pride in the family name they want to see maintained. In effect, our children join us in the legacy process. Practically, the family name comes up in many areas. For example, let's say a younger child is whining. I know—never happens in your family, but we've seen it a few times in ours! I might say to the child, "Are you whining? That's not something we do in our family. Mannings don't whine! Now go back upstairs and come back with a voice that is pleasant, and I'll be happy to listen to what you want. However, I'm not going to listen to that voice!"

A lot has been communicated to the child here. First, he understands I do want to listen to him, just not on those terms. Second, it reinforces he is not being singled out—whining is not acceptable for anyone in our family. Third, it reinforces how to live right within the family structure. Finally, it conveys whining not only hurts him, but it isolates him from the family.

Positively, we make a big deal of any compliment we receive from outside sources about our children. We'll almost always share the compliment in front of as many family members as possible, even if we have to repeat it. "Wow, I was so proud today. Mrs. Sullivan came up to me as I was picking you guys up from school and said, 'McKenzie is such a sweet girl! She helped me pick up after class today without my asking, and she was the only one to do so. She has such a sweet and helpful spirit about her!'" In our home, comments like that are cause for celebration. I'll say something like, "McKenzie, that brings such joy to my heart, not only for you but also for our family. The Mannings will be thought of more highly because you did that!"

This concept works. Kids, without even knowing they're doing it, start to think this way. As they interact with others, they start to realize their actions not only reflect on themselves and God, but on their family as well.

*We want our children to believe their family is a winner, and they're a big part of the team.*

As we've implemented this in our family, God has given our family favor in our church, school, and community. People want us to be a part of things. They want our kids involved in their activities. They trust our family. Our kids see this, and they see it helps open doors in their lives. Further, it builds their hearts to see others praising their siblings and their parents. It's like the feeling you get when your team wins. We want our children to believe their family is a winner, and they're a big part of the team.

Over time, I've seen our children encouraging one another

to act in ways which are in line with the family. The older kids see the value of creating pathways for their younger siblings. Part of their motivation to do well is to make it easier for their siblings to have a pathway to success. They've seen how our family reputation made their lives easier. Now they want to do their part to make that happen for others in the family.

Every once in a while, the older girls will all decide to go see one of the boys' baseball games. It's really a funny event because they sit on the bleachers, right by first or third base, and completely embarrass whichever brother is playing. They rather obnoxiously whoop and holler whenever their brother makes a play, comes up to bat, or even moves in any noticeable way. Their brothers act embarrassed, but inside they're thrilled at the attention. Even the umpires comment on their sisters' display. It's the girls' way of showing that part of the world we are family, and they want to bring honor and favor to the family name.

Mollie has some interesting comments on the concept of the family name, especially since she's the only one who has a different birth father.

**MOLLIE: This subject is one of great value to me. Don isn't my biological father. He married my mom when I was two, but I've been Mollie Manning for as long as I can remember. My name was never legally changed, but until I was married many people knew me as Mollie Manning. It's a name I want to own and a name I want to represent. Growing up, my mom always made "being a Manning" almost like a cool club to be a part of. She began when we were young, reinforcing *who a Manning is*. Some examples: Mannings clean up before they go to bed; Mannings love to play with their little siblings; Mannings are respectful at friends' houses; Mannings pray at the dinner table; Mannings obey; Mannings love Jesus. Sometimes she would reinforce with things we don't do, like Mannings don't whine and Mannings don't hit. She did an amazing job of creating realistic and achievable standards of who the Mannings were and were not to be. This created in us an almost**

subconscious desire to not only become what Mom was speaking over us, but also embrace the calling and contribute to the name. She presented a fun, exciting, come-be-a-part-of-making-our-family-great challenge, and we accepted.

What I love even more about adopting the family name is you get to be greater than yourself, a part of something bigger; you get to celebrate and claim the successes of all Mannings in things you'd never be successful at. Macy is a phenomenal worship leader, and I can't sing to save my life. But I claim that great gift—the Mannings are worship leaders—because of Macy. I brag on the talent the Lord has given her and the talent Macy has used as a Manning every chance I get. McKenzie is this crazy good runner, and I avoid all running; but I claim the Mannings are runners because McKenzie brings that talent to who the Mannings are and what our name means. I could write a lengthy chapter on all the things each person has added to our family name.

While those examples are talents we have, it expands to character qualities, personalities, and, most importantly, how we love the Lord. I've had the privilege of going on a mission trip with all my sisters. There's not a more humbling, yet pride and joy-filled experience, than watching your sibling lead someone to the Lord. To see them fulfill the purpose that comes with holding *the Name* of an adopted son or daughter of the King of Kings, and at the same time add to what it means to be a Manning, is truly an amazing family experience! With this comes great pride in who our family is, which in turn leads to the desire to never tarnish, but always excel, the Manning family name. I kid you not, there were countless times in high school and even more in college when friends asked me to do things, and although I might have wanted to do them, in my mind I knew: (1) That's not how a Manning would act, and (2) I would never want this to be what represents the Manning name.

The family name concept gives us confidence to walk in

the things that we are. Madeline is a prayer warrior and Macy is a worshiper. When I feel weak in prayer and too lazy to worship, I remember those things my sisters have made Mannings to be, and I'm given confidence and energy to be better than I am...because of who they have made Mannings to be!

**MADDOX:** The family calls this concept the *family name,* but I call it "monkey see, monkey do!" As the sisters grew up and made choices, us little brothers were watching them, seeing what it is that makes the Mannings so different. We saw them make good grades, have godly friends, read their Bible, save money, serve families by babysitting, respect Mom and Dad, and love us. All these things showed us this is what Mannings do...it's who we are...so now we do it, too. Get it? Monkey see, monkey do!

One final thought to end this chapter—parents can't be hypocrites here. We must buy into this concept as well. If we tell the kids to be great role models, but Dad is a drunk or Mom throws a fit over the slightest offense, our kids won't buy into the concept. It doesn't mean you have to be perfect, but we as parents must be willing to lead by example more than by lecture. It's a team concept and everyone, especially the parents, needs to participate.

We're in the legacy-building business with our families. It's a great thing for our kids to tap into the idea that the world is bigger than them, and they'll help themselves by helping others. Building a family name into their hearts is a great way to make them think about their actions and turn their hearts towards their siblings and parents.

# END HERE

You did it! You finished the book, and now you have three commitments (I will pursue God, I will build relationships, I will create culture) to filter all your parenting energy through. You're ready to build your Crazy Cool Family!

God has hand-picked YOU to lead your family in an intentional, crazy cool way. No one else is better equipped and gifted to guide your family in this journey of life than you. So, jump in!

The best way we know how to wrap up this book is to do what we do when we end our conferences—we pray over parents. We pray declaring statements of hope, courage, and empowerment. We tell them to print the statements out and post them all over their house—on the mirror, the fridge, in their journal—as reminders of who we are in Christ and the life God has for our family.

We want to do the same for you, our readers. We've prayed these statements over you as well! Before you even read the book, we've prayed for you!

And now it's your turn! Take a moment and declare these statements out loud over yourself and your family. Then print and post them in the well-traveled places of your daily life.

- I am a child of God.
- I hear God's voice clearly.
- With Jesus, we can overcome any family obstacle.
- I love and appreciate my spouse.

- I point my kids to Jesus, and they are amazing.
- My kids can and will be best friends with each other.
- I am an over-the-top encourager to my family.
- I listen, and I am a safe place for my family.
- I intentionally disciple my children.
- My family members are my favorite people in the world.
- God designed the best (Your family name here) family for me.

The Crazy Cool Family journey does not end here! We have a Crazy Cool Family website that we invite you to check out: *crazycoolfamily.com*

We're adding more and new helpful content to this site all the time. It's a way for us to stay connected—sharing this family journey. We look forward to hearing from you! And now...

*"The Lord bless you and keep you; the Lord make his face shine on you and be gracious to you"* (Numbers 6:24-25).

Rethink the Way You Do Family!

# APPENDICES

These six books have helped build our beliefs.
We highly recommend them to you.

For Pursue God
*Waking the Dead*, John Eldredge
*Follow the Cloud*, John Stickl

For Building Relationships
*Sacred Marriage*, Gary Thomas
*Sacred Parenting*, Gary Thomas

For Creating Culture
*Shepherding a Child's Heart*, Tedd Tripp
*A Praying Parent*, Stormie Omartian

# ACKNOWLEDGEMENTS & THANKS

We are so grateful for our parents and siblings. Thanks, Mom and Dad, (Larry, Beth, Gayla, Bob) for deeply loving and supporting us! You laid the foundation from which we have built our family and in turn this ministry to help other families. We would not be who we are today without your initial investment in our lives!

There are so many others to thank for their investment in our journey, but one couple is at the front. Our church founding pastor, Kevin Evans and his wife Lisa, were the couple that put us on the road to a Crazy Cool Family! They invested in us deeply and opened our eyes to God-designed possibilities in our family that were totally unknown to us. We are overwhelmed with gratefulness that God made our paths intertwine at just the right time. The concepts in this book come from decades of influence you have had in our lives!

We thank our seven absolutely amazing children who love the Lord with all their hearts. You have taken everything God has taught us and multiplied it! You are mighty women and men of God and we feel blessed beyond words that God allowed us to be on this journey of life as your parents! You are our best cheerleaders for life, this book, and the Crazy Cool Family ministry. Thank you for loving us well—we love you most!

We are grateful for the thousands of moms and dads that have opened up their lives and allowed us to speak into their hearts and their way of parenting. Thanks so much for your invaluable feedback and your openness to God's leading. Through it, you have shaped how we have built our ministry.

Finally, there are too many friends and ministry partners to name so we would like to thank them all with one big HUG! So many people have prayed for, done life with, listened to, invested in, and cared for us. We are very blessed to have so many godly, kingdom-minded people in our lives.

# ABOUT THE AUTHORS

Don and Suzanne Manning both grew up in Denton, Texas and graduated from the University of North Texas—Don with an accounting degree and Suzanne with a teaching degree. After being set up on a post-college blind date, they have been married for over twenty-five years. In their first year of marriage, they helped launch Valley Creek Church, now a large, multi-site church in Denton County. Don serves as an elder there, and Valley Creek has been a big part of their married lives.

Suzanne began her career as a teacher in the public school system. As more children came along, she was called to stay home and train them up in the way they should go. This past decade she has been serving at Liberty Christian School as a teacher and Minister to Girls. Now she is back home and devotes herself to the Crazy Cool Family ministry.

Don is a CPA and is in the real estate business in the Denton County area. He is the CFO of a property management company and, along with the owner, puts together real estate deals for investors in the community.

Made in the USA
Monee, IL
02 October 2020

43713278R10134